A Guidebook *to* Waking *the* Dead

A GUIDEBOOK TO
WAKING *the* DEAD

EMBRACING THE LIFE GOD HAS FOR YOU

JOHN ELDREDGE

AND

CRAIG MCCONNELL

NELSON IMPACT
A Division of Thomas Nelson Publishers
Since 1798

www.thomasnelson.com

Published in Nashville, Tennessee, by Thomas Nelson, Inc.

Published in association with Yates & Yates, LLP, Attorneys and Counselors, Orange, California.

Unless otherwise noted, Scripture quotations are from the HOLY BIBLE: NEW INTERNATIONAL VERSION®. Copyright © 1973, 1978, 1984 by International Bible Society. Used by permission of Zondervan Publishing House. All rights reserved.

Scripture quotations noted NLT are from the *Holy Bible,* New Living Translation, copyright © 1996. Used by permission of Tyndale House Publishers, Inc., Wheaton, Illinois, 60189. All rights reserved.

Scripture quotations noted NASB are from the NEW AMERICAN STANDARD BIBLE®, Copyright © The Lockman Foundation 1960, 1962, 1963, 1968, 1971, 1972, 1973, 1975, 1977, 1995. Used by permission. (www.Lockman.org)

Scripture quotations noted KJV are from the KING JAMES VERSION.

Scripture quotations noted NKJV are from THE NEW KING JAMES VERSION. Copyright © 1979, 1980, 1982, Thomas Nelson, Inc., Publishers.

Scripture quotations noted MOFFATT are from *The Bible: James Moffatt Translation* by James A. R. Moffatt. Copyright 1950, 1952, 1953, 1954, by James A. R. Moffatt.

Scripture quotations noted The Message are from *The Message* by Eugene H. Peterson, Copyright © 1993, 1994, 1995, 1996, 2000. Used by permission of NavPress Publishing Group. All rights reserved.

Scripture quotations noted NRSV are from the NEW REVISED VERSION of the Bible. Copyright © 1989 by the Division of Christian Education of the National Council of The Churches of Christ in the U.S.A. All rights reserved.

ISBN 0-7852-6309-8

Printed in the United States of America

06 07 08 VG 10 9

CONTENTS

INTRODUCTION

There is more.

No matter what you have known, no matter how precious your life with God has been to date, or how disappointed you've been and elusive he may have seemed . . . there is more available with God. There is so much more.

Now. In this life.

But to discover that "more," we must launch out into deep waters, leave what is familiar, search for new shores. We must learn to live in the rest of reality, which is to say, we must learn to see life spiritually, and we must take seriously the fierce battle for our hearts. We *must* get our hearts back.

Jesus, I want my whole heart back.

That was the prayer that in many ways began this journey for us. Or perhaps it simply brought all the pieces into focus, helped us see what Jesus had been wanting to do all this time. And that is our prayer for you: that through the help of this guidebook, Jesus would restore your heart and bring you into the life he promised to give.

Waking the Dead is revolutionary. One friend who read it said we ought to nail it to the door of the church, like Luther. It opens up for us all a new and much deeper Christianity than most of us have been living. Paul Harvey might call it "the rest of the story." It will probably at some point challenge some cherished notions, or stretch your faith and understanding beyond what you might find comfortable. That's okay—God always does that when he is taking his people into new territory. If you'll remember, the Jews had a pretty hard time accepting Jesus. He seemed outside their preconceived notions of what God was like. But those who did let go of the Law in exchange for the living Son of God found the life they were seeking.

So we encourage you to press on, to open yourself up to some new ways of knowing God and his work in your life. You see, Craig and I have been to those new shores, walked with God there, and we are back to tell you how to find that life and freedom and restoration for yourself. There *is* more.

A few words of counsel on using this guidebook. First (pardon the obvious), you need to read the corresponding chapter in *Waking the Dead* before you jump into the guidebook. For this only makes sense in light of that. Second, take your time. There's no rush. Don't force this into a tight format or program. Third, we encourage you to pray before you read, and do the work we've laid out here. A simple prayer, like Paul prayed, that God "may give you the Spirit of wisdom and revelation, so that you may know him better . . . that the eyes of your heart may be enlightened" (Eph. 1:17–18).

This will forever change your life. In a really good way.

"Further up," as Lewis would say, "and further in."

John Eldredge and Craig McConnell
Colorado
May 2003

TO CLARIFY

Okay . . . I divided *Waking the Dead* into four parts:

> SEEING OUR WAY CLEARLY
> THE RANSOMED HEART
> THE FOUR STREAMS
> THE WAY OF THE HEART

The reason I did so is because each part is so important, so new, and so vital to our lives, I wanted to make sure that you were clearly tracking with me.

So, we're going to include the introductions to each part here in the guidebook as well. If you reread them, they will help you as you go along.

PART ONE

SEEING OUR WAY CLEARLY

*The way through the world
Is more difficult to find than the way beyond it.*
—WALLACE STEVENS

Narrow the road that leads to life, and only a few find it.
—JESUS OF NAZARETH (MATT. 7:14)

There are few things more crucial to us than our own lives.

And there are few things we are less clear about.

This journey we are taking is hardly down the yellow brick road. Then again, that's not a bad analogy at all. We may set out in the light, with hope and joy, but eventually, our path always seems to lead us into the woods, shrouded with a low-lying mist. Where is this abundant life that Christ supposedly promised? Where is God when we need him most? What is to become of us?

The cumulative effect of days upon years that we do not really understand is a subtle *erosion*. We come to doubt our place, we come to question God's intentions toward us, and we lose track of the most important things in life.

We're not fully convinced that God's offer to us *is* life. We have forgotten that the heart is central. And we had no idea that we were born into a world at war. (pp. 1–2)

CHAPTER ONE

ARM YOURSELVES

The thief comes only to steal and kill and destroy; I have come that they may have life, and have it to the full.

—JESUS OF NAZARETH (JOHN 10:10)

HEART MONITOR

Take an inventory before you begin. How are you doing? Where are you right now? What are you feeling . . . thinking . . . wanting? What's your mood?

What's been nagging at you today? Any discouragement . . . distraction? Are you even aware of what's been nipping at your heels?

And are you hopeful, expectant about God using this new material in your life?

What circumstances, pressures, or relational issues could distract you from embracing all God may have for you in this chapter? What would be good to lay down right now in prayer?

Finally, a simple prayer:

Jesus, I ask you now for the Spirit of wisdom and revelation. By your Spirit, guide me through my work here, so that I may know you, really know you, and find the life you offer me. Open the eyes of my heart, Lord. I want all that you have for me here. I want, and ask for, my whole heart back.

A FIRST REACTION

Before we dig in, jot down your first thoughts, emotions, impressions. What did the chapter stir in you? What struck you? Did anything stir a "*yes!*" or an "aha!"?

❋ THE BIG IDEAS

As we said, *Waking the Dead*, if taken seriously, is . . . revolutionary. So as we move along, what we're going to do is help you focus on the Big Ideas, the central truths of each chapter. There are three big ideas in chapter 1:

FIRST, most of us live in a fog, most of the time. Twenty clear days a year. I think I see what's really going on about that often. Wouldn't a little bit of clarity go a long way right now?

SECOND, the offer of Christ is life and that life starts *now*. The glory of God is man fully alive. Now.

THIRD, there *is* something set against us. We are at war. How we've missed this for so long is a mystery. Maybe we've overlooked it; maybe we've chosen not to see. *We are at war.* Until we come to terms with *war* as the context of our days we will not understand life.

Big Idea 1: WE NEED CLARITY

Twenty clear days a year—that sounds about like my life. I think I see what's really going on about that often. The rest of the time, it feels like fog, like the bathroom mirror after a hot shower. You know what I mean. What exactly are you perfectly clear on these days? How about your life—why have things gone the way they have? Where was God in all that? And do you know what you ought to do next, with a deep, settled confidence that it will work out? Neither do I. Oh, I'd *love* to wake each morning knowing exactly who I am and where God is taking me. Zeroed in on all my relationships, undaunted in my calling. But for most of us, life seems more like driving along with a dirty windshield, and then turning into the sun. I can sort of make out the shapes ahead, and I think the light is green. (p. 5)

Can you relate to that sense of being in a fog? When it comes to your life, what exactly *are* you perfectly clear on these days?

Why have things gone the way they have, and where was God in all that? And do you know what you ought to do next, with a deep, settled confidence that it will work out?

Do you wake each morning knowing exactly who you are and where God is taking you? How about this morning?

Are you zeroed in right now in your relationships? What is going on right now in your key relationships—and what will that require of you next?

> Let's start with why life is so dang *hard*. You try to lose a little weight, but it never seems to happen. You think of making a shift in your career, maybe even serving God, but you never actually get to it. Perhaps a few of you do make the jump, but it rarely pans out the way you thought. You try to recover something in your marriage, and your spouse looks at you with a glance that says, "Nice try" or "Isn't it a little late for that?" and the thing actually blows up into an argument in front of the kids. Yes, we have our faith. But even there—maybe *especially* there—it all seems to fall rather short of the promise. There's talk of freedom, and abundant life, of peace like a river and joy unspeakable, but we see precious little of it, to be honest. (p. 5)

Life is hard. Sometimes really hard. Why? I mean, prior to reading the chapter, how have you explained that to yourself?

> *Up until I really came to see the Battle, I just thought life was hard because of sin—you know, "It's a fallen world," and all that. We blew it, and now this is the world we get.*

Make the best of it. Be more grateful. In fact, it was almost a sin to admit it wasn't all that great. Anyhow, that was my theology.

But I think down in my heart I thought life was hard because I just hadn't found the key yet to making it work. Maybe if I try harder, or maybe when I'm more spiritual, or more mature, then things will work out. So, I guess I had my theological explanation, and I had my gut-level understanding. Theology: It's a fallen world. Gut Level: I just can't make it work. (John)

Why is it that, as Tillich said, it's only "here and there in the world and now and then in ourselves" we see any evidence of a new creation? Here and there, now and then. In other words . . . not much. When you stand them side by side, the *description* of the Christian life practically shouted in the New Testament compared with the *actual* life of most Christians, it's . . . embarrassing. Paul sounds like a madman, and we look a little foolish, like children who've been held back a grade. How come nearly every good thing, from taking the annual family vacation to planning a wedding to cultivating a relationship, takes so much work? (pp. 5–6)

In a few honest moments, how *would* you describe your life if you were to stand it beside the description of the Christian life presented in the New Testament? Would you feel embarrassed? Ashamed? Disappointed? And is your experience of the Christian life unfolding in a beautifully hopeful way—or do you feel stuck?

I'm laughing to myself right now because I'm realizing that for years, I thought that the Bible was about "those folks" who lived a long time ago and far, far away and got to have some unique experience with God . . . but now I live here and things are different and I don't really get to have what they had. It's pretty revealing. I didn't think that life was even available. (John)

And right after they made it to Paris, it all fell apart. Craig came down with walking pneumonia; Lori wanted to leave the third day. All sorts of issues in their marriage surfaced, but, since they were with friends, the issues mostly played themselves out in their own thoughts—which tended toward divorce. It wasn't romantic; it was *hard*. Afterward, as we talked on the phone about the whole thing, Lori said, "Life never seems to turn out they way you think it will, about 90 percent of the time." No kidding. Haven't we all got a story that goes with that little bumper sticker? (p. 6)

The story about Craig and Lori's ruined anniversary isn't that uncommon. What plan hasn't worked out in the past year that you were really hoping would—and how did that make you feel?

"Hi . . . it's me." A long silence. "Blaine needs surgery . . . right away."

Hope vanished. I felt that sick-in-the-gut feeling of an imminent free fall, that feeling you get on top of a ladder that's starting to sway under you. All kinds of thoughts and emotions rushed in. *What? Oh, no . . . Not after all this . . . I . . . I thought . . .* My heart was sinking. Despair, betrayal, abandonment by God. Failure on our part to pray enough or believe enough. I felt moments away from a total loss of heart. It seemed inevitable.

These moments aren't a rational, calculated progression of thought; they're more like being tossed out of a raft in a storm. It comes fast and furious, but the pull of the current is always toward a loss of heart. Most of the time we are swept away; we give in, lose heart, and climb out of it sometime later. (pp. 7–8)

The story about my son is far more troubling. I mean, I'm not talking about a vacation—I'm talking about someone I love. What has happened to you, or someone you love, that's caused you to lose heart, be swept away by the storm?

Has God abandoned us? Did we not pray enough? Is this just something we accept as "part of life," suck it up even though it breaks our hearts? (p. 9)

And how did that event with you or someone you loved make you feel? Where did you go with it? Did you feel abandoned? Responsible? Did you just come to accept it?

After a while, the accumulation of event after event that we do not like and do not understand erodes our confidence that we are part of something grand and good, and reduces us to a survivalist mind-set. I know, I know—we've been told that we matter to God. And part of us partly believes it. But life has a way of chipping away at that conviction, undermining our settled belief that he means us well. I mean, if that's true, then why didn't he_____? Fill in the blank. Heal your mom. Save your marriage. Get you married. Help you out more. (p. 9)

Go ahead and expand on what God hasn't done that he *could* have done for you. What hasn't he prevented that he *could* have prevented?

And what do you make of that? How have you understood what you just wrote about? What's the explanation for it?

> Either (*a*) We're blowing it, or (*b*) God is holding out on us. Or some combination of both, which is where most people land. Think about it. Isn't this where *you* land, with all the things that haven't gone the way you'd hoped and wanted? Isn't it some version of "I'm blowing it"? in that it's your fault, you could have done better, you could have been braver or wiser or more beautiful or something? Or "God is holding out on me," in that you know he *could* come through, but he hasn't come through—and what are you to make of that? (p. 9)

Take the two events you wrote about—one on the level of a ruined vacation, and the other in response to the deeper crisis involving someone you love. How have you handled those? What have they done to your relationship with God?

So which is your more common reaction to understanding the trials, disappointments, and blows of your life? Is it (*a*) You are blowing it, (*b*) God is holding out on you, or (*c*) some combination of both? What I'm asking for is some honesty here. There are the "right" answers, the ones we might offer in a church service or Bible study, and then there are our real answers, the ones that come from our hearts when we are being absolutely honest.

For me, it's definitely (c) a combination of I'm blowing it and God just isn't coming through. (John)

Big Idea 2: THE OFFER IS LIFE

The glory of God is man fully alive. (Saint Irenaeus)

When I first stumbled across this quote, my initial reaction was . . . *You're kidding me. Really?* I mean, is that what you've been told? That the purpose of God—the very thing he's staked his reputation on—is your coming fully alive? (p. 10)

How could the opposite be true? Could it bring glory to God for his precious children to be pinned down with guilt and shame and who knows what, broken, hurting, barely making it through life? What does that do for his reputation?

I turned to the New Testament to have another look, read for myself what it is Jesus said he offers. "I have come that they may have life, and have it to the full" (John 10:10). Wow. That's different from saying, "I have come to forgive you. Period." Forgiveness is awesome, but Jesus says here he came to give us *life*. Hmmm. Sounds like ol' Irenaeus might be on to something. "I am the bread of life" (John 6:48). "Whoever believes in me, as the Scripture has said, streams of living water will flow from within him" (John 7:38). The more I looked, the more this whole theme of life jumped off the pages. I mean, it's *everywhere*.

> Above all else, guard your heart,
> for it is the wellspring of life. (Prov. 4:23)

> You have made known to me the path of life. (Ps. 16:11)

> In him was life, and that life was the light of men. (John 1:4)

> Come to me to have life. (John 5:40)

> Tell the people the full message of this new life. (Acts 5:20)

> I am still confident of this:
> I will see the goodness of the LORD
> in the land of the living. (Ps. 27:13) (pp. 10–11)

So, what do *you* make of these passages? What did Jesus mean when he promised us life?

TO CLARIFY

Okay . . . I know this whole question of "what has God promised us in *this* life?" is fraught with problems. It's a question that's got heresy on both sides. So, let me make a few things clear:

I am not advocating a "name it and claim it" theology, whereby we can have anything and everything we want if we just claim it in Jesus' name. After all, Jesus said, "In this world you will have trouble" (John 16:33).

Nor am I advocating a "prosperity" doctrine that claims God wants everyone to be rich and healthy. "The poor you will always have with you" (Matt. 26:11).

What I *am* saying is that Christ does not put his offer of Life to us totally in the future. That's the other mistake. "'I tell you the truth,' Jesus said to them, 'no one who has left home or wife or brothers or parents or children for the sake of the kingdom of God will fail to receive many times as much *in this age* and, in the age to come, eternal life'" (Luke 18:29–30, emphasis added).

Jesus doesn't locate his offer to us only in some distant future, after we've slogged our way through our days here on earth. He talks about a life available to us *in this age*. So does Paul: "Godliness has value for all things, holding promise *for both the present life* and the life to come" (1 Tim. 4:8, emphasis added).

There is a Life available to us now. Let's find it.

Big Idea 3: WE ARE AT WAR

The thief comes only to steal and kill and destroy; I have come that they may have life, and have it to the full. (John 10:10)

Have you ever wondered why Jesus married those two statements? Did you even know he spoke them at the same time? (pp. 12–13)

Did you? Now that you do know, what do you make of it?

We are at war.

How we've missed this for so long is a mystery to me. Maybe we've overlooked it; maybe we've chosen not to see. *We are at war.* I don't like that fact any more than you do, but the sooner you come to terms with it the better hope you have of making it through to the life you do want. This is not Eden. You probably figured that out. This is not Mayberry, this is not *Seinfeld*'s world; this is not *Survivor.* The world in which we live is a combat zone, a violent clash of kingdoms, a bitter struggle unto the death. I am sorry if I'm the one to break this news to you: you were born into a world at war, and you will live all your days in the midst of a great battle, involving all the forces of heaven and hell and played out here on earth.

Where *did* you think all this opposition was coming from? (p. 13)

Well . . . where did you think all the opposition and assault in your life was coming from?

I think over the course of my life I have cycled through most of the options. I've blamed it on political systems and policies. I've blamed it on people. I've even blamed it on God. But for the majority of my twenty-five years as a Christian, in all the churches I've gone to, in all the books I've read, in all the people I've known, very few have ever taken the Enemy or the Battle seriously. Even though we might say we know Satan is out there, very, very few Christians ever ascribe their struggles to a direct attack by spiritual forces of darkness.

The idea of a thief trying to steal my life wasn't even on my radar. (John)

Earlier in the Story, back in the beginning of our time on earth, a great glory was bestowed upon us. We all—men and women—were created in the image of God. Fearfully and wonderfully made, fashioned as living icons of the bravest, wisest, most stunning Person who ever lived. Those who have ever seen him fell to their knees without even thinking about it, as you find yourself breathless before the Grand Canyon or the Alps or the sea at dawn. That glory was shared with us; we were, in Chesterton's phrase, "statues of God walking about in a Garden," endowed with a strength and beauty all our own. All that we ever wished we could be we were—and more. We were fully alive.

> So God created man in his own image,
> > in the image of God he created him;
> > male and female he created them. (Gen. 1:27)

> When I look at the night sky and see the work of your fingers—
> > the moon and the stars you have set in place—
> what are mortals that you should think of us,
> > mere humans that you should care for us?
> For you made us only a little lower than God,
> > and you crowned us with glory and honor. (Ps. 8:3–5 NLT)

I daresay we've heard a bit about original sin, but not nearly enough about original glory, which comes *before* sin and is deeper to our nature. We were crowned with glory and honor. Why does a woman long to be beautiful? Why does a man hope to be found brave? Because we remember, if only faintly, that we were once more than we are now. (pp. 13–14)

Clearly, our story does not begin with sin. It begins in Genesis 1, not Genesis 3. Is that a new thought to you? What does it begin to open up, to realize that you were created to be glorious?

The reason you doubt there could be a glory to your life is because that glory has been the object of a long and brutal war.

For lurking in that Garden was an Enemy. This mighty angel had once been glorious as well, the captain of the Lord's hosts, beautiful and powerful beyond compare. But he rebelled against his Creator, led a great battle against the forces of heaven, and was cast down. Banished from his heavenly home, but not destroyed, he waited for an opportunity to take his revenge. (p. 14)

You must understand: the Evil One hates the glory of God . . . wherever it exists.

Unable to overthrow the Mighty One, he turned his sights on those who bore his image. He lied to us about where true life was to be found, and we believed him. We fell, and "our glory faded," as Milton said, "faded so soon." Or as David lamented, "You turn my glory into shame" (Ps. 4:2). (p. 14)

I'll bet you've blamed all your failings on yourself. You've probably just assumed that the sole reason you aren't the glorious creation of God today is because of your sin. But we were seduced, tricked, betrayed. Yes, we chose to disobey, but Scripture makes clear that an Enemy *staged* our downfall. Does this help you to realize that there is a battle against you?

But God did not abandon us, not by a long shot. I think even a quick read of the Old Testament would be enough to convince you that *war* is a central theme of God's activity. There is the Exodus, where God goes to war to set his captive people free . . .

Then it's war to get *to* the promised land . . . Then it's war to get *into* the promised land—Joshua and the battle of Jericho, all that. After the Jews gain the promised land, it's war after war to *keep* it . . . Are you getting the picture?

Many people think the theme of war ends with the Old Testament. Not at all. Jesus says, "I did not come to bring peace, but a sword" (Matt. 10:34). In fact, his birth involved another bloody battle in heaven . . .

The birth of Christ was an act of war, an *invasion* . . . And when he returns, I might point out, Jesus will be mounted on a steed of war, with his robe dipped in blood, armed for battle (Rev. 19:11–15).

War is not just one among many themes in the Bible. It is *the* backdrop for the whole Story, the context for everything else. (pp. 14–16)

Okay, react now to that. War is not just one among many themes in the Bible. It is *the* backdrop for the whole story. What does it begin to help you see?

> Right now I'm realizing that maybe everything we're going through with Sam right now—what the world would write off as "adolescence"—might be more battle than I thought. I mean, the pull to come down hard on him, and his pull to just back away and sulk—look at the fruit of it. Satan would love to separate us. (John)

You may not like this explanation of the world we have. In fact, that sigh you just felt— *Oh, does it have to be this way? I'm not sure I really want to deal with this*—that is a sign of the battle right there. The last thing the Enemy wants you to do is stand up and fight for your life. If you come alive, why . . . that would bring glory to God.

In the course of this chapter, and especially as you get closer to embracing the truth that we are in a great Battle, have you felt that other reaction—that sigh, that sense of *Oh, does it have to be this way? I'm not sure I really want to deal with this*? If so, where did you think that came from?

But if you would live by the truth, this is the one the Scriptures offer you.

> Until we come to terms with war as the context of our days we will not understand
> life. We will misinterpret 90 percent of what is happening around us and to us. It will

be very hard to believe that God's intentions toward us are life abundant; it will be even harder not to feel that somehow we are just blowing it . . .

. . . That day is coming, *later*, when the lion shall lie down with the lamb and we'll beat swords into plowshares. For now, it's bloody battle.

. . . You won't understand your life, you won't see clearly what has happened to you or how to live forward from here, unless you see it as *battle*. A war against your heart. And you are going to need your whole heart for what's coming next. I don't mean what's coming next in the story I'm telling. I mean what's coming next in the life you're living. (pp. 17–18)

How deeply do you want the freedom and life that Christ promised? Deeply enough to *fight* for it?

And so, where is your heart as you end this chapter? Can you put into a sentence or two what God has said to you through this chapter?

What was the most stirring idea in this chapter for you?

What questions or desires do you want to take to God?

To bring this time to a close, pray.

CHAPTER TWO

THE EYES OF THE HEART

I pray also that the eyes of your heart may be enlightened.
—THE APOSTLE PAUL (EPH. 1:18)

HEART MONITOR

Take an inventory before you begin. How are you doing? Where are you right now? What are you feeling . . . thinking . . . wanting? What's your mood?

What's been nagging at you today? Any discouragement . . . distraction? Are you even aware of what's been nipping at your heels?

And are you hopeful, expectant about God using this new material in your life?

What circumstances, pressures, or relational issues could distract you from embracing all God may have for you in this chapter? What would be good to lay down right now in prayer?

Finally, a simple prayer:

Jesus, I ask you now for the Spirit of wisdom and revelation. By your Spirit, guide me through my work here, so that I may know you, really know you, and find the life you offer me. Open the eyes of my heart, Lord. I want all that you have for me here. I want, and ask for, my whole heart back.

A FIRST REACTION

What was the effect of this chapter upon you? Write out your impressions: any new or challenging thoughts, emotions or stirrings in your heart, or even perhaps something you intend to do.

A MYTHIC PARABLE

Two men are seated across from each other in a dark room. Outside, a thunderstorm rages in the night, shaking the old house to its foundations. Flashes of lightning are dimmed by heavy curtains that muffle the sound of the rain falling in a deluge, as if it remembers the time it flooded the earth and longs to do it again. The curtains have been drawn because it is a *secret* meeting. This is the first time these men have ever met, though they have been searching for each other most of their lives. Not a moment too soon, their destinies have crossed. One of them, a tall black man dressed all in black, carries the aura of a spiritual master. The younger man, trying his best to conceal the fact that he is frightened and uncertain, might become his disciple. It all depends on a decision.

MORPHEUS: I imagine that right now you're feeling a bit like Alice, tumbling down the rabbit hole?

NEO: You could say that.

MORPHEUS: I can see it in your eyes. You have the look of a man who accepts what he sees because he's expecting to wake up. Ironically, this is not far from the truth. Do you believe in fate, Neo?

NEO: No.

MORPHEUS: Why?

NEO: Because I don't like the idea that I'm not in control of my life.

MORPHEUS: I know exactly what you mean. Let me tell you why you're here. You're here because you know something. *What* you know you can't explain. You feel it. You've felt it your entire life. There's something wrong with the world. You don't know what it is. But it's there, like a splinter in your mind, driving you mad. It is this feeling that has brought you to me. Do you know what I'm talking about?

NEO: The Matrix?

MORPHEUS: Do you want to know what it is?

[*Hesitantly, Neo nods his assent.*]

MORPHEUS: The Matrix is everywhere. It is all around us. Even now in this very room. You can see it when you look out your window, or when you turn on your television. You can feel it when you go to work, when you go to church, when you pay your taxes. It is the world that has been pulled over your eyes to blind you from the truth.

NEO: What truth?

MORPHEUS: That you are a slave, Neo. Like everyone else you were born into bondage, into a prison that you cannot taste or smell or touch. A prison for your mind. Unfortunately, no one can be told what the Matrix is. You must see it for yourself.

[*In each of his open palms, held forth as an offering, the older man is holding two capsules, one red, the other blue. He is offering the younger man a chance at the truth.*]

MORPHEUS: This is your last chance. After this, there is no turning back. You take the blue pill—the story ends, you wake up in your bed and you believe . . . whatever you want to believe. You take the red pill—you stay in Wonderland and I show you how deep the rabbit hole goes. (pp. 19–21)

What does it stir in you? Does it open up some aspect of the Christian life to you . . . or some aspect of your life?

✿ THE BIG IDEAS

FIRST, things are not what they seem. There is a whole lot more going here than meets the eye. We live in two worlds—or better, in one world with two parts, one part that we can see and one part that we cannot. We are urged, for our own welfare, to act as though the unseen world (the rest of reality) is in fact more weighty and more real and more dangerous than the part of reality we can see.

SECOND, we are at war. This is a world at war. Something large and immensely dangerous is unfolding all around us; we are caught up in it.

THIRD, you have a crucial role to play. You are not what you think you are. There is a glory to your life that your Enemy fears, and he is hell-bent on destroying that glory before you act on it.

Big Idea 1: THINGS ARE NOT WHAT THEY SEEM

Read the sections "Seeing with the Heart" and "Mythic Reality" on pages 23–26.

. . . when Jesus comes to town, he speaks in a way that will get past all our intellectual defenses and disarm our hearts. He tells a certain kind of story. As Chesterton said, "I am concerned with a certain way of looking at life, which was created in me by the fairy tales, but has since been ratified by the mere facts." And the best stories of all, the ones that bring us the Eternal Truths, they always take the form of parable, or, sometimes we say, fairy tale. Better still to call them *myths*. (p. 24)

Myths contain the deepest truths of all.

I am not using *myth* in a technical way, referring to ancient Greek mythology. I am using it more broadly, more inclusively, to mean "a story that brings you a glimpse of the eternal" or "any story that awakens your heart to the deep truths of life." (p. 25)

Why do stories awaken your heart? What are some of your favorite stories Christ told?

Neo takes the red pill; Lucy steps through the wardrobe; Aladdin rubs the lamp; Elisha prays that the eyes of his servant would be opened; Peter, James, and John follow Jesus up to the Mount of Transfiguration. And all of them discover that there is far more going on here than meets the eye. The film *The Matrix* is a parable, a metaphor, far closer to reality and to your life than you probably have been led to believe. And the question Morpheus asks of Neo is a question the Scriptures ask of us: Do you *want* to see? (p. 21)

How willing are you to take the "red pill," to have God show you realities of life that you may never have seen? Giving this some thought, do you find such an offer exciting, a bit frightening, or perhaps both? Scribble out your thoughts.

Hey, give me the red pill and a glass of water. I'll take it . . . but not without reservations. After all, my self-protective tendency is to fully understand all that I'm signing up for. I might see some pretty gnarly stuff about myself, my heart, God. I have a hunger to know and have everything God is willing to show and give me, yet I want to retain the option of whether or not to live out of such knowledge

. . . a head-under-the-pillows approach: show me just the good stuff . . . please! And yet, deeper than that, I do want it all! (Craig)

What do all the great stories and myths tell us? What do they have in common? What are they trying to get across? Wherever they may come from, whatever their shape might be, they nearly always speak to us Three Eternal Truths. First, these stories are trying to remind us that *things are not what they seem.* There is a whole lot more going on here than meets the eye. (p. 26)

Is the idea that there is far more going on here than meets the eye new to you, or is it a reminder of a truth you've either forgotten or set aside?

On the personal level, no, it's not new. I've been aware of the reality that more is going on in my internal, unseen life than meets the eye. I've seen how easy it is to fake a relationship with God. As a pastor I got pretty good at appearing to have an intimacy with Christ I wasn't really living in. And yet, when it comes to my day-to-day living, the routines and notably mundane affairs of my life leave me wondering if anything "more" is going on at all. On the level of my worldview, I've accepted, theologically, that there are unseen evil powers and forces, but I've lived most of my Christian life as if nothing of the kind existed. So on that level, yes, this is all new. (Craig)

To Clarify

Giving it a bit more thought, this reality of "more going on than meets the eye" is seen throughout Scripture:

What appears to be simply a serpent is the Enemy of God and of our hearts with the agenda to destroy you.

That sweet newborn baby in the manger is the Lion of Judah, the Son of God about to battle for our freedom, our lives . . . our salvation.

An Angel of Light may, in fact, be Satan . . . There are *false* prophets who look real, hirelings *posing* as shepherds, kind words *masking* a vicious heart (Ps. 55:21), and some pretty "godly" looking people who are anything but godly on the inside (Matt. 23:25–28).

After the tornado sets her down, Dorothy *wakes* and steps out of her old farmhouse to find herself in a strange new world, a land of Munchkins and fairies and wicked witches . . .

Alice falls through the rabbit hole into Wonderland. Adonos *wakes* to the sound of water and discovers a stream running right through his bedroom . . .

Neo is *awakened* from the death-sleep of the Matrix to discover that the time is not 1999, but 2199, and the world he thought was real is actually a massive deception cast upon the human race to keep them prisoners. Jacob falls into a dream under the desert stars and sees a ladder "resting on the earth, with its top reaching to heaven, and the angels of God . . . ascending and descending on it" (Gen. 28:12). He wakes, more awake than he's ever been in his life, thanks to the dream, and realizes for the first time that there is more going on around him than he ever imagined. "Surely the LORD is in this place, and I was not aware of it" (28:16). (pp. 26–27)

So many stories involve an awakening of some kind. Does your story? How certain are you that you're not in some kind of a soul or spiritual malaise, fog, or slumber now, not really seeing things as they are? Are there areas in your life that seem to be under a fog . . .

to be missing clarity (relational difficulties, internal peace or direction, unbroken habits/addictions, ongoing confusion about God and his will/direction for your life . . .)?

Just today I woke up from a season of being covered with a blanket of condemnation over some financial choices. This thing has been suffocating me for quite a while, but I didn't see it until it culminated in a sleepless night of shame and unceasing accusation ("You're a failure," "You'll be bankrupt, lose the house and your wife," "You'll never make it"). Until it hit the fan I didn't realize the deadening impact it has had . . . over the last thirty years! (Craig)

Isn't this the very lesson of the Emmaus Road? . . .

. . . The story is so human, so true to our lives. What is so wonderful and hopeful and—because *we* know how it turns out—also cracks me up is how they did not see. *They just didn't get it.* (pp. 27–28)

To what extent has your posture been "Seeing is believing," and thus ruled out the possibility of there being unseen spiritual realities? To what degree would you describe yourself as being "slow of heart to believe"? If you wouldn't describe yourself in that way, how would you?

I became a Christian through a pretty wacky ministry. I left it after several chaotic years. My ensuing theological studies supported my desire to get as far away from that subjective emotional mystical stuff as I could. For many years following, my posture was "Seeing is believing." But even if I saw something, I wouldn't believe it if it didn't fit with my antisupernatural presuppositions about life. Yes, I've been slow of heart to believe a lot of things about God and how he works; about myself and my heart; about the world and evil. (Craig)

They ignored the secret of the burning heart. For the story goes on, as you may remember, and the mysterious Companion begins to chide them for being "slow of heart to believe" as he reminds them of the writings of the prophets, all the ancient wisdom. They invite him to supper, and after another bit of feigning about needing to move on, he does come in.

When he was at the table with them, he took bread, gave thanks, broke it and began to give it to them. Then their eyes were opened and they recognized him, and he disappeared from their sight. They asked each other, "Were not our hearts burning within us while he talked with us on the road and opened the Scriptures to us?" (Luke 24:30–32) (p. 28)

Have you ever had an experience where your heart was burning within you? What makes or would make your heart burn? What's it burning for right now? If you've never experienced your heart burning within, why do you think that is?

Yes, every time I see the final two scenes of Braveheart my heart surfaces and affirms the reality of my deep true and core love for God. I know the truest thing about me is that I love the Lord my God with all my heart. At the same time (an interesting connection!) I also feel the severe weightiness of my heart's desire to take the gospel in all its life-giving power to those who are captives, prisoners, and brokenhearted. More and more I'm aware of these passions that truly define me. Oh, may they govern my life! (Craig)

This is precisely what the Bible has warned us about all these years: that we live in two worlds—or better, in one world with two halves, one part that we can see and one part that we cannot. We are urged, for our own welfare, to act as though the unseen world (the rest of reality) is, in fact, more weighty and more real and more dangerous than the part of reality we can see. The lesson from the story of the Emmaus Road—the lesson the whole Bible is trying to get across—begins with this simple truth: things are not what they seem. There is more going on here than meets the eye. Far more. That is Eternal Truth Number One. (p. 29)

Do you begin to see it?

Big Idea 2: WE ARE AT WAR

The Second Eternal Truth brought to us comes like a broken message over the radio, or an urgent e-mail from a distant country, telling us that some great struggle or quest or battle is well under way. May even be hanging in the balance. When the four children stumble into Narnia, the country and all its lovely creatures are imprisoned under the spell of the White Witch and have been for a hundred years. In another story, Jack and his mother are starving and must sell their only cow. Frodo barely makes it out of the Shire with his life and the ring of power. In the nick of time he learns that Bilbo's magic ring is the One Ring, that Sauron has discovered its whereabouts, and the Nine Black Riders are already across the borders searching for the little hobbit with deadly intent. The future of Middle Earth hangs on a thread.

Darth Vader just about has the universe under his evil fist when a pair of droids fall into the hands of Luke Skywalker. Luke has no idea what is unfolding, what great deeds have been done on his behalf, or what will be required of him in the battle to come. Sitting in a sandstone hut with old Ben Kenobi—he does not know this is the great Jedi warrior Obi-Wan Kenobi—Luke discovers the secret message from the princess. "This is our most desperate hour. Help me, Obi-Wan Kenobi. You're my only hope."

Again, this is *exactly* what the Scriptures have been trying to wake us up to for years. "Wake up, O sleeper . . . Be very careful, then, how you live . . . because the days are evil" (Eph. 5:14–16). (pp. 29–30)

According to this verse, why are we to "wake up"? And what does "because the days are evil" mean?

Christianity isn't a religion about Sunday school and potluck suppers, being nice, holding car washes, sending our secondhand clothes off to Mexico. This is a world at war. Something large and immensely dangerous is unfolding all around us, we are caught up in it, and above all we doubt we have been given a key role to play. Do you think I'm being too dramatic? (p. 30)

We're at war! Does life feel like combat to you, or is John being too dramatic? If the war metaphor doesn't fit, what does?

It hasn't always. I resisted this idea for as long as I could—it seemed to be giving too much attention to evil. But the more I observed and listened to others' stories, as well as my own, I couldn't ignore the carnage, the casualties, wounds, scars, death, and destruction, all the collateral damage that mark the trail of our Adversary and the lives of those around me.

I see the Enemy's assault on my wife, my daughters, and closest friends. I feel his venomous rage at my walking more intimately with God. War is the most accurate metaphor. (Craig)

In what ways does your life feel as though you're living in a war zone? What have been the losses, the wounds, the casualties in your life as a result of the war? What battles are you currently facing?

Whom have you blamed for the war: God? Yourself? Others? The Adversary?

Read the passage regarding Daniel's crisis in Daniel 10.

Something has happened that Daniel doesn't understand. I think we can all relate to that. We don't understand about 90 percent of what happens to us, either. Daniel is troubled. He sets out to get an answer. But three weeks of prayer and fasting produce no results. What is he to conclude? If Daniel were like most people, by this point he'd probably be headed toward one of two conclusions: *I'm blowing it*, or *God is holding out on me*. He might try confessing every sin and petty offense in hopes of opening up the lines of communication with God. Or he might withdraw into a sort of disappointed resignation, drop the fast, and turn on the television. In an effort to hang on to his faith, he might embrace the difficulty as part of "God's will for his life." He might read a book on "the silence of God." That's the way the people I know handle this sort of thing.

And he would be dead wrong.

On the twenty-first day of the fast an angel shows up, out of breath. In a sort of apology the angel explains to Daniel that God had actually dispatched him in answer to Daniel's prayers the very first day he prayed—three weeks ago. (There goes the whole unanswered prayer thesis, right out the window.) *Three weeks ago?* What is Daniel to do with that? "The very first day? But . . . I've . . . I mean, thank you so very much, and I don't want to seem ungrateful, but . . . where have you *been?*" You haven't blown it, Daniel, and God isn't holding out on you. The angel goes on to explain that he was locked in hand-to-hand combat with a mighty fallen angel, a demonic power of dreadful strength, who kept him out of the Persian kingdom for three weeks, and he finally had to go get Michael (the great archangel, the captain of the Lord's hosts) to come and help him break through enemy lines. "Now I am here, in answer to your prayer. Sorry it's taken so long." (pp. 31–32)

What conclusions can you draw from this story about *your* life, some of the difficulties you may face?

How much of what you've just written is new to you? How must you begin to view your world differently?

There it is—Eternal Truth Number Two: *this is a world at war.* We live in a far more dramatic, far more dangerous story than we ever imagined. The reason we love *The Chronicles of Narnia* or *Star Wars* or *The Matrix* or *The Lord of the Rings* is that they are telling us something about our lives that we never, ever get on the evening news. Or from most pulpits. *This is our most desperate hour.* Without this burning in our hearts, we lose the meaning of our days. It all withers down to fast food and bills and voice mail and who really cares anyway? Do you see what has happened? The essence of our faith has been stripped away. The very thing that was to give our lives meaning and *protect us*—this way of seeing—has been lost. Or stolen from us. Notice that those who have tried to wake us up to this reality were usually killed for it: the prophets, Jesus, Stephen, Paul, most of the disciples, in fact. Has it ever occurred to you that someone was trying to shut them up?

Things are not what they seem. This is a world at war. (p. 32)

What does the thought that this is a world at war stir in you? What governing beliefs does it disrupt? (That Christ has established peace on earth? That Christ has secured our victory against evil? That the Christian life is primarily worship, love, and saving souls, not battle? Etc. . . .)

Big Idea 3: THE WEIGHT OF YOUR GLORY

Last, but not least, not by a long shot, *every mythic story* shouts *to us that in this desperate hour we have a crucial role to play.* That is the Third Eternal Truth, and it happens to be the one we most desperately need if we are ever to understand our days. For most of his life, Neo sees himself only as Thomas Anderson, computer programmer for a large software corporation. As the drama really begins to heat up and the enemy hunts him down, he says to himself, "This is insane. Why is this happening to me? What did I do? I'm nobody. I didn't do anything." A very dangerous conviction . . . though one shared by most of you, my readers. What he later comes to realize—and not a moment too soon—is that he is "the One" who will break the power of the Matrix.

Frodo, the little Halfling from the Shire, young and naive in so many ways, "the most unlikely person imaginable," is the Ring Bearer. He, too, must learn through dangerous paths and fierce battle that a task has been appointed to him, and if he does not find a way, no one will. Dorothy is just a farm girl from Kansas, who stumbled into Oz not because she was looking for adventure but because someone had hurt her feelings and she decided to run away from home. Yet she's the one to bring down the Wicked Witch of the West. Joan of Arc was also a farm girl, illiterate, the youngest in her family, when she received her first vision from God. Just about everyone doubted her; the commander of the French army said she should be taken home and given a good whipping. Yet she ends up leading the armies in war.

You see this throughout Scripture: a little boy will slay the giant; a loudmouthed fisherman who can't hold down a job will lead the church, and a whore with a golden heart is the one to perform the deed that Jesus asked us all to tell "wherever the gospel is preached throughout the world" (Mark 14:9). Things are not what they seem. *We* are not what we seem. (pp. 32–33)

Do you feel embarrassed (maybe even like you are sinning) to consider that *you have a glory* and *a vital role to play?* Why is this so hard to believe?

It's simple, really. I don't believe this because my failures, sin, immaturity, track record, weaknesses, wounds, and life circumstances loom greater in my mind than the work of Christ, my identity in Christ, and his call on my life. It's that simple and it's tragic. (Craig)

As Lewis wrote, "The value of . . . myth is that it takes all the things we know and restores to them the rich significance which has been hidden by 'the veil of familiarity.'" You are not what you think you are. There is a glory to your life that your Enemy fears, and he is hell-bent on destroying that glory before you act on it. This part of the answer will sound unbelievable at first; perhaps it will sound too good to be true; certainly, you will wonder if it is true for you. But once you begin to see with those eyes, once you have begun to know it is true from the bottom of your heart, it will change everything. (pp. 33–34)

What role would you love to play?

In a moment that may feel sinfully self-centered and embarrassingly arrogant, think about what it would look like for you to live in your glory. (This may take a little more time for personal reflection.) If you were to live in your full glory, why would the Enemy have good reason to fear you?

> This is hard to do, and more so to share with others (the accusation is that it's vain and sinful glory-seeking). The enemy will fear me because my glory is to be a Warrior-Shepherd whose life and words draw others to Christ in such a deep and lasting way that they, in turn, draw multitudes to Christ in an irreversible and wonderful way. If I'm close to what God's design and desire are, I'm a threat that needs to be reckoned with. (It sounds so . . . arrogant, and yet, it is what seems to be written upon my heart.) (Craig)

Did you find it easy or difficult to answer this question? Why or why not? Where did those thoughts regarding your glory come from? Could they very well be God's desire and design for you, written upon your heart?

The story of your life is the story of the long and brutal assault on your heart by the one who knows what you could be and fears it. (p. 34)

Looking back over your life, what has the Enemy done to assault your heart and to "take you out"? Have you seen this before?

My father's death, when I was an infant, provided a springboard for the Enemy's lies to convince me that I was lacking critical necessities of life. His message, "You don't have what it takes to survive—your destiny will be failure, isolation, shame, and total rejection," was convincing motivation for me to run, isolate, medicate, horde . . . and fake it. I viewed my "heart" as inadequate, dirty, as dead tissue . . . of absolutely no use. (Craig)

Seeing Satan's strategy against you stirs what emotions in your heart? What would you like God to do for you at this moment?

To be used powerfully by God, in whatever way he chooses and calls me to be a part of the sword that destroys the works of the devil. (Craig)

TO CLARIFY

Listen to this prayer, one of many deliverance prayers penned by John Chrysostom, archbishop of Constantinople. It might help you to express your thoughts to your enemy:

Satan, the Lord rebukes you by his frightful name! Shudder, tremble, be afraid, depart, be utterly destroyed, be banished! You who fell from heaven and together with you all evil spirits . . . Depart swiftly from this creature of the Creator Christ our God! And be gone from this servant of God, from his mind, from his soul, from his heart, from his reins, from his senses, from all his members, that he might become whole and sound and free, knowing God.

Amen!

About halfway through their journey—following a great deal of hardship and facing a good deal more—Frodo's devoted friend and servant, Sam Gamgee, wonders out loud: "I wonder what sort of tale we've fallen into." Sam is at that moment thinking mythically. He is wondering in the right way. His question assumes that there *is* a story; there is something larger going on. He also assumes that they have somehow tumbled into it, been swept up into it. This is exactly what we've lost. Things happen to you. The car breaks down, you have a fight with your spouse, or you suddenly figure out how to fix a problem at work. What is *really* happening? David Whyte says that we live our lives under a pale sky, "the modern loss of dramatic sensibility, the lost sense that we play out our lives as part of a greater story."

What sort of tale have I fallen into? is a question that would help us all a great deal if we wondered it for ourselves. After my friend Julie saw *The Fellowship of the Ring*, she turned to the girl with her and whispered, "We've just gotten a clearer view of reality than we usually see." Yes—that's the kind of "seeing" we need; that *is* our reality. What grabbed me was the theatrical trailer for the film. In a brilliantly crafted three-minute summary, the preview captures the essential mythic elements of the story. As scene after scene races before the eyes of the viewer, and Gandalf describes the tale, these lines cross the screen:

> Fate has chosen him.
> A Fellowship will protect him.
> Evil will hunt him.

Yes—that's it. That is the life Christianity is trying to explain to the world. Better, that is the reality into which Christianity is the door. If we could believe that about our lives, and come to *know* that it is true, everything would change. We would be so much more able to interpret the events unfolding around us, against us. We would discover that task that is ours alone to fulfill. We would find our courage. The hour is late and you are needed. So much hangs in the balance. Where *is* your heart? (pp. 34–35)

And so, where is your heart as you end this chapter? Can you put into a sentence or two what God has said to you through this chapter?

What was the most stirring idea in this chapter for you?

What questions or desires do you want to take to God?

To bring this time to a close, pray.

CHAPTER THREE

THE HEART OF ALL THINGS

Above all else, guard your heart,
for it is the wellspring of life.

—KING SOLOMON (PROV. 4:23)

You are never a great man when you have more mind than heart.

—BEAUCHENE

HEART MONITOR

Take an inventory before you begin. How are you doing? Where are you right now? What are you feeling . . . thinking . . . wanting? What's your mood?

What's been nagging at you today? Any discouragement . . . distraction? Are you even aware of what's been nipping at your heels?

And are you hopeful, expectant about God using this new material in your life?

What circumstances, pressures, or relational issues could distract you from embracing all God may have for you in this chapter? What would be good to lay down right now in prayer?

Finally, a simple prayer:

Jesus, I ask you now for the Spirit of wisdom and revelation. By your Spirit, guide me through my work here, so that I may know you, really know you, and find the life you offer me. Open the eyes of my heart, Lord. I want all that you have for me here. I want, and ask for, my whole heart back.

A First Reaction

What was the effect of this chapter upon you? Write out your impressions: any new or challenging thoughts, emotions or stirrings in your heart, or even perhaps something you intend to do.

A MYTHIC PARABLE

On her journey down the yellow brick road—a journey, may I remind you, that grows more dangerous every step she takes—Dorothy meets a number of strange sights. She befriends the Scarecrow, and later the two of them come upon a lumberjack made of tin, standing utterly still in the forest, his ax frozen in midair. At first, he seems unable to speak. Coming closer, they discover that he is trying to say something after all. *Oil . . . can*. After a bit more misunderstanding and misinterpretation, they get the oil can to the joints of his mouth, only to find that he can speak as well as any man, but that he was rusted. Once he is freed from his prison, he begins to tell them his story.

Now the movie left out a crucial point, which the author gave in his original fairy tale. The Tin Woodman had once been a *real* man, who had been in love with a beautiful maiden. It was his dream to marry her, once he could earn enough money to build them a cottage in the woods. The Wicked Witch hated his love, and she cast spells upon the man that caused him injury, so that one by one his limbs needed to be replaced with artificial ones, made of tin. At first it seemed an advantage, for his metal frame allowed him to work nearly as powerfully as a machine. With a heart of love and arms that never tired, he seemed sure to win.

"I thought I had beaten the Wicked Witch then, and I worked harder than ever; but I little knew how cruel my enemy could be. She thought of a new way to kill my love for the beautiful Munchkin maiden, and made my axe slip again, so that it cut right through my body, splitting it into two halves. Once more the tinner came to my help and made me a body of tin. Fastening my tin arms and legs and head to it, by means of joints, so that I could move around as well as ever. But alas! I now had no heart, so that I lost all my love for the Munchkin girl, and did not care whether I married her or not . . .

"My body shone so brightly in the sun that I felt very proud of it and it did not matter now if my axe slipped, for it could not cut me. There was only one danger—that my joints would rust; but I kept an oil-can in the cottage and took care to oil myself whenever I needed it. However, there came a day when I forgot to do this, and, being caught in a rainstorm, before I had thought of the danger my joints had rusted, and I was left to stand in the woods until you came to help me.

"It was a terrible thing to undergo, but during the year I stood there I had time to think that the greatest loss I had known was the loss of my heart. While I was in love I was the happiest man on earth; but no one can love who has not a heart, and so I am resolved to ask Oz to give me one. If he does, I will go back to the Munchkin maiden and marry her."

Both Dorothy and the Scarecrow had been greatly interested in the story of the Tin Woodman, and now they knew why he was so anxious to get a new heart. "All the same," said the Scarecrow, "I shall ask for brains instead of a heart; for a fool would not know what to do with a heart if he had one." "I shall take the heart," returned the Tin Woodman; "for brains do not make one happy, and happiness is the best thing in the world." (L. Frank Baum, *The Wonderful Wizard of Oz*) (pp. 36–38)

What does the story stir in you? Does it open up some aspect of the Christian life to you . . . or some aspect of your life?

❧ THE BIG IDEAS

FIRST, the heart is central. I find it almost hard to believe a case must be made that the heart is . . . well, at the heart of it all. Of life. Of each person. Of God. And of Christianity.

SECOND, the point of all living is love. Somewhere down inside we know it's true; we know love is the point. We know if we could truly love, and be loved, and never lose love, we would finally be happy. Loving requires a heart alive and awake and free.

THIRD, Christ's mission can be summed up as to give you back your heart and set you free.

Big Idea 1: OUR HEARTS ARE CENTRAL

"It was a terrible thing to undergo, but during the year I stood there I had time to think that the greatest loss I had known was the loss of my heart. While I was in love I was the happiest man on earth; but no one can love who has not a heart, and so I am resolved to ask Oz to give me one. If he does, I will go back to the Munchkin maiden and marry her."

. . . The Enemy knows how vital the heart is, even if we do not, and all his forces are fixed upon its destruction. For if he can disable or deaden your heart, then he has effectively foiled the plan of God, which was to create a world where love reigns. By taking out your heart the Enemy takes out *you*, and you are essential to the Story. (pp. 37–38)

When have you lost heart, and what impact did it have upon your intimacy with God and with others? Why, if you lose heart, is God's plan foiled?

I'm just emerging from a long season of my heart for ministry being practically destroyed. Having been assaulted by men-with-no-chests posing as godly leaders, I lost all passion, desire, and interest in my call as a pastor. What has startled me is that I didn't notice I had lost heart; my cynicism, the blues, and a lack of desire seemed justified and appropriate given the situation. I didn't really see myself as missing something vital until Christ began to restore my heart this last month or so. I have a pulse again in the core of my being! This has been a very renewing month or two!

God has restored my heart . . . though, from my perspective, a lot of time has been lost, he will redeem the lost years. His plan has not been foiled. (Craig)

When we no longer live from the heart, we often live simply for efficiency, productivity, safety, busyness, or niceness. What occupied your focus in those seasons? What occupies your focus now?

To some degree is your heart still weak, deadened, wounded, or disabled in some ways? Describe the current state of your heart.

Perhaps another way to answer the question is to fill in the blanks:

In my walk with God: I wish my heart were more _____ instead of _____.

In my relationship with my spouse or close friends: I long for my heart to be more _____ instead of _____.

When it comes to living life, I wish my heart were more _____ than _____.

To Clarify

Some indicators of losing heart:

- Personal conversation with God and the pleasure of sweet communion with him is infrequent.
- In your relationship with God you most often experience shame, condemnation, a sense of being disqualified or unable to please him.
- Your walk with God is reduced to a focus on external behaviors (with principles, lists of do's and don'ts) rather than internal realities (desires, fears, emotions).
- Most of your Christian activity is done under pressure.
- You lose sight of the way things really are.

- You don't see yourself as having a crucial role in God's Story.
- You no longer believe or live as if the world is at war.
- Life becomes exclusively routine, mundane . . . you live in a malaise or fog bank.
- Work or career is mostly drudgery.
- You have little passion for beauty, adventure.
- You rarely belly laugh or weep.
- Men are bored, have accepted or hidden addictions/habits (compulsive behaviors, excessive behaviors, pornography, anger, etc.).
- Women are too busy, have accepted or hidden addictions/habits (compulsive behaviors, excessive behaviors, volunteering, romance stories, etc.).
- You become preoccupied with . . . you, your needs, desires, wounds.

The heart is central. That we would even need to be reminded of this only shows how far we have fallen from the life we were meant to live—or how powerful the spell has been. The subject of the heart is addressed in the Bible more than any other topic—more than works or service, more than belief or obedience, more than money, and even more than worship. Maybe God knows something we've forgotten. But of course—all those other things are matters of the heart. Consider a few passages:

Love the LORD your God with all your heart and with all your soul and with all your strength. (Deut. 6:5) [Jesus called this the greatest of all the commandments—and notice that the heart comes first.]

Man looks at the outward appearance, but the LORD looks at the heart. (1 Sam. 16:7)

Where your treasure is, there your heart will be also. (Luke 12:34)

Trust in the LORD with all your heart
and lean not on your own understanding. (Prov. 3:5)

Your word I have treasured in my heart,
That I may not sin against You. (Ps. 119:11 NASB)

These people honor me with their lips,
  but their hearts are far from me. (Matt. 15:8)

For the eyes of the LORD range throughout the earth to strengthen those whose hearts are fully committed to him. (2 Chron. 16:9) (pp. 39–40)

Have you seen the heart as central to Scripture? If not, what else did you think was central?

I hadn't.

Though Scripture referred to the heart, I always viewed it the way I do my spleen: though I am not really sure what it does, I assume it's important, wouldn't want to be without it, and I've gotten along pretty well without paying any attention to it. What was central was my will. Every problem could be solved if I wanted, really wanted, and chose to obey Scripture. All the commands and exhortations could be lived out, adhered to if I chose to obey. Knowing Scripture and choosing to obey it were central to living the Christian life. I fear I was better at obedience than I was at loving God. (Craig)

Think about your work life for a moment. Why are so many people bored or frustrated with their jobs? Why do they dread Monday morning and "thank God it's Friday"? Their hearts are not in their work. Far from it. However they arrived at what they're doing with their lives, it wasn't by listening to their hearts. The same holds true for their love life. Why do so many relationships fail? Because one or both partners no longer have a heart for making it work. On and on it goes. Why are so many people struggling with depression and discouragement? They've lost heart. Why can't we seem to break free of our addictions? Because somewhere along the way, in a moment of carelessness or desperation, we gave our hearts away, and now we can't get them back.

There is no escaping the centrality of the heart. God knows that; it's why he made it the central theme of the Bible, just as he placed the physical heart in the center of the human body. The heart is central; to find our lives, we must make it central again.

. . . The apostle Paul drives this home when he states: "That if you confess with your mouth, 'Jesus is Lord,' and believe in your heart that God raised him from the dead, you will be saved. For it is with your heart that you believe and are justified" (Rom. 10:9–10). Read that again more slowly. "It is with your *heart* that you believe." Where does saving faith come from? The heart. Which raises a troubling reality for all of us: you do not belong to God, you are not a Christian at all, until you engage your heart, believe *with your heart*. Jesus said the same when, in a moment of frustration with his own people, he cried,

> For this people's heart has become calloused;
>   they hardly hear with their ears,
>   and they have closed their eyes.
> Otherwise they might see with their eyes,
>   hear with their ears,
>   *understand with their hearts*
> and turn, and I would heal them. (Matt. 13:15, emphasis added)

The mind is a faculty, and a magnificent one at that. But the heart is the dwelling place of our *true* beliefs. (pp. 40–41, 45–46)

What seems to be emphasized more in your world today: believing with your heart, or knowing the right stuff in your head?

I'm in between worlds, moving the full eighteen inches from my head to my heart. (Craig)

This battle for the heart is going to take all the courage you can muster. Heaven forbid you leave that heart behind. (p. 47)

Describe how you would live if your heart was central.

For me, I think the faint echoes I hear when I am still or reflective would increase in volume. These simple and pure inclinations to love, listen, heed, follow, touch, confront, care, worship, and enjoy would fill my day. I'd pause more for beauty, press into new adventures, and labor with clarity and focus. I'd catch little opportunities to enjoy life, encourage others, and lean into Christ. Just writing this out rouses my desire to live like this. God, I yearn to live from my heart! (Craig)

Big Idea 2: THE POINT OF ALL LIVING

Everything you love is what makes a life worth living. Take a moment, set the book down, and make a list of all the things you love. Don't edit yourself; don't worry about prioritizing or anything of that sort. Simply think of all the things you love. Whether it's the people in your life or the things that bring you joy or the places that are dear to you or your God, you could not love them if you did not have a heart . . . Loving requires a heart alive and awake and free.

Of all the things that are required of us in this life, which is the most important? What is the real point of our existence? Jesus was confronted with the question point-blank one day, and he boiled it all down to two things: loving God and loving others. Do this, he said, and you will find the purpose of your life. Everything else will fall into place. Somewhere down inside we know it's true; we know love is the point. We know if we could truly love, and be loved, and never lose love, we would finally be happy. Gerald May wrote, "We are created by love, to live in love, for the sake of love." And is it even possible to love *without* your heart?

The heart is the connecting point, the meeting place between any two persons. The kind of deep soul intimacy we crave with God and with others can be experienced only from the heart. (pp. 47–48)

How deep are your relationships with others these days? Do you even have time for relationship?

I have a couple of deeply meaningful relationships, a larger circle of very close friends, and an even wider circle of friends. I am blessed yet hope for more. While I'm comfortable where things are, in some ways it seems that I'm relationally lazy or settling for less. I have the time but seem to invest my energy in less-demanding pursuits (sports, free reading, newspapers, idle time, organizing, futzing around). (Craig)

What does your answer say about what you think the point of all living is?

Christians have spent their whole lives mastering all sorts of principles, done their duty, carried on the programs of their church . . . and never known God intimately, heart to heart . . . "I never knew you" (Matt. 7:23) . . . Attend a class and take in information; then use that information to change the way you live. None of that will bring you into intimacy with God, just as taking a course on anatomy won't help you love your spouse. "You will find me," God says, "when you seek me with all your heart" (Jer. 29:13). (pp. 48–49)

As Oswald Chambers said, "So that is what faith is—God perceived by the heart." What does intimacy with God look like to you?

Do you define it in a very personal way or by the fulfillment of duties and adherence to principles?

What's kept it from being richer than it is?

What more can be said, what greater case could be made than this: to find God, you must look with all your heart. To remain present to God, you must remain present to your heart. To hear his voice, you must listen with your heart. To love him, you must love with all your heart. You cannot be the person God meant you to be, and you cannot live the life he meant you to live, unless you live from the heart. (p. 49)

What does that stir in you?

I want that . . . living more and more from my heart. It's true in my life: if Christ hasn't captured my full heart, I'll look for something that promises to. (Craig)

Big Idea 3: CHRIST'S MISSION

Christ did not die for an idea. He died for a person, and that person is you. But there again, we have been led astray. Ask any number of people why Christ came, and you'll receive any number of answers, but rarely the real one. "He came to bring world peace." "He came to teach us the way of love." "He came to die so that we might go to heaven." "He came to bring economic justice." On and on it goes, much of it based in a partial truth. But wouldn't it be better to let him speak for himself?

Jesus steps into the scene. He reaches back to a four-hundred-year-old prophecy to tell us why he's come. He quotes from Isaiah 61:1, which goes like this:

> The Spirit of the Sovereign LORD is on me,
> because the LORD has anointed me
> to preach good news to the poor.
> He has sent me to bind up the brokenhearted,

> to proclaim freedom for the captives
> and release from darkness for the prisoners. (p. 50)

Put into your own words the good news of Christ's mission given in this passage.

The meaning of this quotation has been clouded by years of religious language and ceremonial draping. What is he saying? It has something to do with good news, with healing hearts, with setting someone free. That much is clear from the text. Permit me a translation in plain language:

> God has sent me on a mission.
> I have some great news for you.
> God has sent me to restore and release something.
> And that something is you.
> I am here to give you back your heart and set you free.

. . . He chose this passage above all others; this is the heart of his mission. Everything else he says and does finds its place under this banner. I am here to give you back your heart and set you free. *That* is why the glory of God is man fully alive: it's what he said he came to do. (pp. 50–51)

What if that were true? Have you tasted *that* ministry of God? Would you want it?

How we've overlooked this is one of the great mysteries of our times. It is simply diabolical, despicable, downright *evil* that the heart should have become so misunderstood, maligned, feared, and dismissed. But there is our clue again. The war we are in would explain so great a loss. This is the *last* thing the Enemy wants you to know. His plan from the beginning was to assault the heart, just as the Wicked Witch did to the Tin Woodman. Make them so busy, they ignore the heart. Wound them so deeply, they don't want a heart. Twist their theology, so they despise the heart. Take away their courage. Destroy their creativity. Make intimacy with God impossible for them. (p. 51)

Has busyness kept you from paying attention to your heart and the hearts around you?

> *Yes—a busyness that has the scent of importance or substance but is more accurately labeled "distraction." It keeps me from giving the attention to my heart it needs. I haven't treated my heart well for many years. (Craig)*

Have wounds made you not want a heart?

Has your theology encouraged you to dismiss the heart?

Of course your heart would be the object of a great and fierce battle. It is your most precious possession. Without your heart you cannot have God. Without your heart you cannot have love. Without your heart you cannot have faith. Without your heart you cannot find that work you were meant to do. In other words, without your heart you cannot have *life*. (p. 52)

And so, where is your heart as you end this chapter? Can you put into a sentence or two what God has said to you through this chapter?

What was the most stirring idea in this chapter for you?

What questions or desires do you want to take to God?

To bring this time to a close, pray.

PART TWO

THE RANSOMED HEART

"The time is coming," declares the LORD,
   "when I will make a new covenant
with the house of Israel
   and with the house of Judah.
It will not be like the covenant
   I made with their forefathers
when I took them by the hand
   to lead them out of Egypt,
because they broke my covenant,
   though I was husband to them," declares the LORD.
"This is the covenant I will make with the house of Israel
   after that time," declares the LORD.
"I will put my law in their minds
   and write it on their hearts.
I will be their God,
   and they will be my people." (Jer. 31:31–33)

I will give you a new heart and put a new spirit in you; I will remove from you your heart of stone and give you a heart of flesh. And I will put my Spirit in you and move you to follow my decrees and be careful to keep my laws. (Ezek. 36:26–27)

This we now know: The heart is central. It matters—deeply. When we see with the eyes of the heart, which is to say, when we see mythically, we begin to awaken and what we discover is that things are not what they seem. We *are* at war. We must fight for the life God intends for us, which is to say, we must fight for our heart, for it is the wellspring of that life within us.

Standing in the way of the path to life—the way of the heart—is a monstrous barrier. It has stopped far too many pilgrims dead in their tracks, for far too long. There is a widespread belief among Christians today that the heart is desperately wicked—even after a person comes to Christ.

It is a crippling belief.

And it is untrue. (pp. 53–54)

CHAPTER FOUR

RANSOMED AND RESTORED

Create in me a clean heart, O God.

—KING DAVID (PS. 51:10 NKJV)

I will give you a new heart.

—GOD (EZEK. 36:26)

HEART MONITOR

Take an inventory before you begin. How are you doing? Where are you right now? What are you feeling . . . thinking . . . wanting? What's your mood?

What's been nagging at you today? Any discouragement . . . distraction? Are you even aware of what's been nipping at your heels?

And are you hopeful, expectant about God using this new material in your life?

What circumstances, pressures, or relational issues could distract you from embracing all God may have for you in this chapter? What would be good to lay down right now in prayer?

Finally, a simple prayer:

Jesus, I ask you now for the Spirit of wisdom and revelation. By your Spirit, guide me through my work here, so that I may know you, really know you, and find the life you offer me. Open the eyes of my heart, Lord. I want all that you have for me here. I want, and ask for, my whole heart back.

A FIRST REACTION

What was the effect of this chapter upon you? Write out your impressions: any new or challenging thoughts, emotions or stirrings in your heart, or even perhaps something you intend to do.

A MYTHIC PARABLE

Now Beauty feared that she had caused his death. She ran throughout the palace, sobbing loudly. After searching everywhere, she recalled her dream and ran into the garden toward the canal, where she had seen him in her sleep. There she found the poor Beast stretched out unconscious. She thought he was dead. Without concern for his horrifying looks, she threw herself on his body and felt his heart beating. So she fetched some water from the canal and threw it on his face.

Beast opened his eyes and said, "You forgot your promise, Beauty. The grief I felt upon having lost you made me decide to fast to death. But I shall die content since I have the pleasure of seeing you one more time."

"No, my dear Beast, you shall not die," said Beauty. "You will live to become my husband. I give you my hand, and I swear that I belong only to you from this moment on. Alas! I thought that I only felt friendship for you, but the torment I am feeling makes me realize that I cannot live without you."

Beauty had scarcely uttered these words when the castle radiated with light. Fireworks and music announced a feast. These attractions did not hold her attention, though. She returned her gaze to her dear Beast, whose dangerous condition made her tremble. How great was her surprise when she discovered that the Beast had disappeared, and at her feet was a prince more handsome than Eros himself, who thanked her for putting an end to his enchantment. (pp. 55–56)

What does the story stir in you? Does it open up some aspect of the Christian life to you . . . or some aspect of your life?

❋ THE BIG IDEAS

FIRST, something has gone wrong with the human race and we know it. Better said, something has gone wrong *within* the human race. Most of the misery we suffer on this planet is the fruit of the human heart gone bad. We all desperately need transformation—a new heart.

SECOND, something deep and profound happened *to* us in the death of Christ. Remember—the heart is the problem. God understands this better than anyone, and he goes for the root. God promised in the new covenant to "take away your heart of stone." Christ removes our hearts of stone.

THIRD, just as we received our sinful nature from Adam, so we now receive a good and holy nature from Christ. We have new hearts. Our hearts are *good*.

Big Idea 1: WE HAVE A DESPERATE NEED

It is the deepest and most wonderful of all mythic truths . . . A creature that no one could bear to look upon is transformed into a handsome prince. That which was dark and ugly is now glorious and good. Is it not the most beautiful outcome of any story to be written? Perhaps that is because it is the deepest yearning of the human heart. (p. 56)

What about the stories you love? What happens to the hearts of the main characters? Are they transformed? Revealed to be good in the end? Do you accept that this is your story as well?

In your own words, why do we need to be transformed? What's the problem with the human race? How has that problem been apparent in your life?

Are you aware of a yearning for transformation, a true, deep, and lasting change? If so, describe your yearning.

If not, is it because everything is really quite good with you? What would stir a desire for transformation?

Yes, I am. When I live on autopilot, which is usually when life isn't presenting any notable challenges, my yearning for change takes a back burner. However, in moments of stillness and reflection, a glorious time of worship, or under the weight of some burden, I am acutely aware of a seemingly desperate hunger for more. I do crave for God to continue the transformation of my pettiness, impatience, posing, distrust, living beyond my means, eating, and doubting of his call on my life. I yearn to be a more loving husband, engaging father, courageous friend . . . I want to be free and alive in ways Christ offers that I have yet to seize . . . and I will, in time. (Craig)

Have you tried to transform your inner life and your external behaviors, and if so, with what success? Do you want more?

There have been some changes I've been able to make; however, there are areas in my life I've tried to transform time and time again for years. I mean, look at my bookshelf . . . anyone want some self-help books that didn't help? (Craig)

Scripture could not be more clear on this. Yes, God created us to reflect his glory, but barely three chapters into the drama we torpedoed the whole project. Sin entered the picture and spread like a computer virus . . .

Any honest person knows this. We know we are not what we were meant to be . . . Most of the world religions concur on this point. Something needs to be done.

. . . The problem is not in our behavior; the problem is *in us.* As Jesus said, "For *out of the heart* come evil thoughts, murder, adultery, sexual immorality, theft, false testimony, slander" (Matt. 15:19, emphasis added). We don't need an upgrade. We need transformation. We need a miracle. (pp. 58–59)

What exactly is the problem that's in us?

Paul refers to Jesus as the Last Adam and the Second Man (1 Cor. 15:45–47). Why is this important? Because of what happened through the *First* Adam.

Our first father, Adam, and our first mother, Eve, were destined to be the root and trunk of humanity. What they were meant to be, we were meant to be: the kings and queens of the earth, the rulers over all creation, the glorious image bearers of a glorious God. They were statues of God walking about in a Garden, radiant Man and Woman, as we were to be. Our natures and our destinies were bound up in theirs. Their choices would forever shape our lives, for good or for evil. It is deep mystery, but we see something of a hint of it in the way children so often follow in the steps of their parents. Haven't you heard it said, "He has his father's temper," or "She has her mother's wit"? As the old saying goes, the fruit doesn't fall far from the tree. In fact, we call them family trees, and Adam and Eve are the first names on the list. (p. 59)

Kings and queens of the earth, rulers over all creation, the glorious image bearers of a glorious God? Describe God's intention for you from the beginning, before the Fall. How is *that* different from your life? What shifted?

Our first parents chose, and it was on the side of evil. They broke the one command, the only command God gave to them, and what followed you can watch any night on the news. The long lament of human history. Something went wrong in their hearts, something *shifted*, and that shift was passed along to each of us . . . Paul makes clear in Romans, "Sin entered the world through one man . . . through the disobedience of the one man the many were made sinners" (5:12, 19). Of course, I am simply restating the doctrine of original sin, a core tenet of Christianity essential to Scripture. (pp. 59–60)

It's easy to rag on Adam, but how have you, over the years, essentially made the same choice? How about this week?

I have chosen to eat from the tree of euphoria, choosing the pursuit of peace, pleasure, and superficial contentment over the submission of those desires to God. I'll eat a bag of Cheetos in times of anxiety instead of turning to God. I've chosen to be *lord over my financial resources, insisting on controlling our assets. I smile, act nice, and present a spiritual maturity that's simply not true.*

This week . . . huh? This week I've turned to my wife, subtly pressuring her to validate and affirm me in ways only God can. Yuck! (Craig)

But that is not the end of the Story, thank God. The First Adam was only "a pattern of the one to come" (Rom. 5:14). He would foreshadow another man, the head of a new race, the firstborn of a new creation, whose life would mean transformation to those who would become joined to him: "For just as through the disobedience of the one man [Adam] the many were made sinners, so also through the obedience of the one man [Christ, the Last Adam] the many will be made righteous" (Rom. 5:19).

. . . In the fifth chapter of the famous book of Romans, Paul asks, Was Adam effective? Did his life have far-reaching consequences? We all know it did. It was devastating. He goes on to say, Well, then, the consequences of Christ, the Last Adam, were even greater: "For if, by the trespass of the one man, death reigned through that one man, *how much more* will those who receive God's abundant provision of grace and of the gift of righteousness reign in life through the one man, Jesus Christ" (Rom. 5:17, emphasis added). (pp. 60–61)

Do the traits of the First Adam seem more a part of your life than those from the Second Adam—or is it vice versa?

Less so now . . . I wish I had been the father I am now when my daughters were infants. Looking back, I see so much less of the fruit of Christ, the Second Adam, in my life then. I'd say the same in my marriage; twenty-seven years ago, though a Christian, I reflected more of the First Adam's traits (an incredible lack of love, as I now understand it . . . Thank God both he and Lori have been merciful and patient). In another fifteen years I'll no doubt see fewer of Adam's traits and more of Christ's. May it be so, dear Jesus. (Craig)

Big Idea 2: CHRIST REMOVES OUR HEARTS OF STONE

Jesus of Nazareth was sentenced to death by a vain puppet of the Roman government acting as district governor of Jerusalem. He was nailed to a cross by a handful of Roman soldiers who happened to be on duty, and left there to die. He died somewhere around three o'clock in the afternoon on a Friday. Of a broken heart, by the way. And we call it Good Friday, of all strange things, because of what it effected. An innocent man, the Son of God, bleeding for the sins of the world . . . To lose us was too great a pain for God to bear, and so he took it upon himself to rescue us. The Son of God came "to give his life as a ransom for many" (Matt. 20:28). (p. 61)

What's Christ's motive in rescuing/ransoming you?

You have been ransomed by Christ. Your treachery is forgiven. You are entirely pardoned for every wrong thought and desire and deed. This is what the vast majority of Christians understand as the central work of Christ for us. And make no mistake about it—it is a deep and stunning truth, one that will set you free and bring you joy. For a while.

But the joy for most of us has proven fleeting because we find that we need to be forgiven again and again and again. Christ has died for us, but we remain (so we believe) deeply marred. It actually ends up producing a great deal of guilt. "After all that Christ has done for you . . . and now you're back here asking forgiveness *again*?" To be destined to a life of repeating the very things that sent our Savior to the cross can hardly be called *salvation*. (pp. 61–62)

Has your perception of the gospel been primarily, perhaps even exclusively, a message of forgiveness? As good as that is, isn't more needed if we hope to live the life God designed and we desire?

Pretty much. I have clung to the offer of forgiveness; I've gotten well versed in asking for it. The truth and implications of such a stunning offer can occupy my thoughts and worship for many, many years. And yes, more is needed and wanted. I cannot read the Gospels and New Testament without aching for all that's available to me through Christ . . . The package is full of gracious and wonderful provisions: life (really alive from the inside out), freedom (from sin, the world, and the devil), passion (for God, his commandments, others, as well as life and all its beauty and adventure), power (to live life, to have an impact, to rescue others from darkness and sin). (Craig)

Think of it: you are a shadow of the person you were meant to be. You have nothing close to the life you were meant to have. And you have no real chance of becoming that person or finding that life. However, you are forgiven. For the rest of your days you will fail in your attempts to become what God wants you to be. You should seek forgiveness and try again. Eventually shame and disappointment will cloud your understanding of yourself and your God. When this ongoing hell on earth is over, you will die, and you will be taken before your God for a full account of how you didn't measure up. But you will be forgiven. After that, you'll be asked to take your place in the choir of heaven. This is what we mean by *salvation.* (p. 62)

How close is this to your experience of Christianity? How inviting would this gospel be to your unbelieving friends?

This is the gospel I've had preached to me for years . . . and preached for years. Truth be known, this is the gospel that I and most of my unbelieving friends found very difficult to embrace. Where's the life!? As a pastor, I saw our church grow not from people coming to Christ but from disenchanted believers transferring from one church to another. (Craig)

The good news is . . . that is *not* Christianity. There is more. *A lot more.* And that more is what most of us have been longing for most of our lives.

. . . It's not just that the Cross did something *for* us. Something deep and profound happened *to* us in the death of Christ. Remember—the heart is the problem. God understands this better than anyone, and he goes for the root. God promised in the new covenant to "take away your heart of stone." How? By joining us to the death of Christ. Our nature was nailed to the cross with Christ; we died there, with him, in him. Yes, it is a deep mystery—"deep magic" as Lewis called it— but that does not make it untrue. "The death he died, he died to sin once for all . . . In the same way, count yourselves dead to sin" (Rom. 6:10–11). Jesus was the Last Adam, the end of that terrible story.

You've been far more than forgiven. God has removed your heart of stone. You've been delivered of what held you back from what you were meant to be. You've been rescued from the part of you that sabotages even your best intentions. Your heart has been circumcised to God. Your heart has been set free. (pp. 62–63)

React . . .

Yes! Yesss!! Yesssss!!! Thank you, God! I am yours . . . totally, completely . . . body, soul, and spirit. You have me! (Craig)

Big Idea 3: CHRIST OFFERS US A NEW HEART

Most people assume that the Cross *is* the total work of Christ. The two go hand in hand in our minds—Jesus Christ and the Cross; the Cross and Jesus Christ. The Resurrection is impressive, but kind of . . . an afterthought. It was needed, of course, to get him out of the grave. Or the Resurrection is important because it proves Jesus was the Son of God. His death was the *real* work on our behalf. The Resurrection is like an epilogue to the real story; the extra point after the touchdown; the medal ceremony after the Olympic event. You can see which we think is more important. What image do we put on our churches, our Bibles, our jewelry? The cross is the symbol of Christianity worldwide. (pp. 63–64)

What importance has the resurrection of Christ had in your life? What have the implications of the Resurrection been for you?

In the past, the Resurrection assured me that I, too, in some future time, would rise from the dead and enjoy eternal life. It also was a huge apologetic tool to convince non-Christians of the Deity and the claims and promises of Christ Jesus. Just writing this out, I realize how sterile and removed from my day-to-day living it was. It's embarrassing to admit that my conscious awareness and appreciation of the Resurrection was practically nonexistent. (Craig)

The cross was never meant to be the only or even the central symbol of Christianity.

That you are shocked by what I've just said only proves how far we've strayed from the faith of the New Testament. The cross is not the sole focal point of Christianity. Paul says so himself: "And if Christ has not been raised, our preaching is useless and so is your faith . . . If Christ has not been raised, your faith is futile; you are still in your sins" (1 Cor. 15:14, 17).

. . . The early Christian church symbolized the Resurrection, healings, and miracles because the church thought those things were central. The reason the first and closest friends of Jesus focused on miracles, healings, and hopeful aspects of the faith like the Ascension and the Resurrection was simply because those are what God himself wants us to focus on. *Those are the point.* Those make Christianity such very good news. A dead man is not a great deal of help to us; a dead God is even worse. But life, real life, the power of God to *restore* you . . . now that's a whole nother matter. (pp. 64–65)

Why are the Resurrection and Ascension such good news?

We say Christ died for us, and that is true. But Christ was also *raised* for us. His resurrection is as much for us as his death was.

> For if, by the trespass of the one man [the First Adam], death reigned through that one man, how much more will those who receive God's abundant provision of grace and of the gift of righteousness *reign in life* through the one man, Jesus Christ. (Rom. 5:17, emphasis added)

> We were therefore buried with him through baptism into death in order that, just as Christ was raised from the dead through the glory of the Father, we too may live a new life . . . In the same way, count yourselves dead to sin but alive to God in Christ Jesus. (Rom. 6:4, 11)

> But because of his great love for us, God . . . made us alive with Christ. (Eph. 2:4–5)

Remember now—Adam was *a pattern* of the One to come. He was the root and trunk of our family tree. Our hearts fell when he fell. We received our sinful nature from him. So we now receive a *new* nature and a *new* heart from Christ, our Second Man. We have been made alive with the life of Christ. Just as we received our sinful nature from Adam, so we now receive a good and holy nature from Christ. It has always been God's plan not just to forgive you, but to restore you: "Make the tree good and its fruit will be good" (Matt. 12:33).

. . . Let me try this again. The new covenant has two parts to it: "I will give you a new heart and put a new spirit in you; I will remove from you your heart of stone and give you a heart of flesh" (Ezek. 36:26). God removed your old heart when he circumcised your heart; he gives you a new heart when he joins you to the life of Christ. That's why Paul can say "count yourselves dead to sin" *and* "alive to God in Christ Jesus" (Rom. 6:11). (pp. 65–67)

List the qualities you think are characteristic of our hearts of stone.

1.

2.

3.

4.

Now list the qualities you think are characteristic of our new hearts.

1.

2.

3.

4.

Which list has been done away with? Cross it out!

> The story of the Incarnation is the story of a descent and resurrection . . . one has the picture of a diver, stripping off garment after garment, making himself naked, then flashing for a moment in the air, and then down through the green, and warm, and sunlit water into the pitch black, cold, freezing water, down into the mud and slime, then up again, his lungs almost bursting, back again to the green and warm and sunlit water, and then at last out into the sunshine, holding in his hand the dripping thing he went down to get. This thing is human nature. (C. S. Lewis, "The Grand Miracle")
>
> The Resurrection affirms the promise Christ made. For it was life he offered to give us: "I have come that they may have life, and have it to the full" (John 10:10). We are saved by his life when we find that *we are able to live* the way we've always known we should live. We are free to be what he meant when he meant us. You have a new life—the life of Christ. And you have a new heart. Do you know what this means? Your heart is good. (p. 67)

If your heart *is* good, what hope do you have for living the life you desire and God designed?

Allow me one more proof.

> Each person knows that now his *body* is the temple of God: "Do you not know that your body is a temple of the Holy Spirit, who is in you, whom you have received from God?" (1 Cor. 6:19). Indeed it is. "Don't you know that you yourselves are God's temple and that God's Spirit lives in you?" (1 Cor. 3:16). Okay—each of us is now the temple of God. So where, then, is the Holy of Holies?
>
> Your heart.
>
> . . . Paul teaches us in Ephesians that "Christ may dwell in your hearts through faith" (3:17). God comes down to dwell in us, *in our hearts.* Now, we know this: God cannot dwell where there is evil. "You are not a God who takes pleasure in evil; with you the wicked cannot dwell" (Ps. 5:4). Something pretty dramatic must have happened in our hearts, then, to make them fit for the dwelling place of a holy God. (p. 68)

Pause and reflect upon the reality that God dwells in you. Write out your thoughts. How does that impact how you view yourself, others? Do you find this hard to believe? Why?

It's really almost beyond my ability to comprehend because I am aware of so much in my life that isn't Godlike, holy, pure, without sin or stain. How could he dwell in me? I haven't ever embraced this reality, really; for God to indwell me says I'm in-dwell-able by the most high and holy almighty God . . . Whoa. There's something different about me for that to happen! (Craig)

To Clarify

From Man's standpoint the most tragic loss suffered in the Fall was the vacating of this inner sanctum by the Spirit of God. At the far-in hidden center of man's being is a bush fitted to be the dwelling place of the Triune God. There God planned to rest and glow with moral and spiritual fire. Man by his sin forfeited this indescribably wonderful privilege and must now dwell there alone. For so intimately private is the place that no creature can intrude; no one can enter but Christ, and He will enter only by the invitation of faith. "Behold, I stand at the door, and knock: if any man hear my voice, and open the door, I will come in to him, and will sup with him, and he with me" (Rev. 3:20 KJV).

By the mysterious operation of the Spirit in the new birth, that which is called by Peter "the divine nature" enters the deep-in core of the believer's heart and establishes residence there. "If any man have not the Spirit of Christ, he is none of his," for "the Spirit itself beareth witness with our spirit, that we are the children of God" (Rom. 8:9, 16 KJV). Such a one is a true Christian, and only such. Baptism, confirmation, the receiving of the sacraments, church membership—these mean nothing unless the supreme act of God in regeneration also takes place. (A. W. Tozer, *Man: The Dwelling Place of God*)

Of course, none of this can happen for us until we give our lives back to God. We cannot know the joy or the life or the freedom of heart I've described here until we surrender our lives to Jesus and surrender them totally. Renouncing all the ways we have turned from God in our hearts, we forsake the idols we have worshiped and given our hearts over to. We turn, and give ourselves body, soul, and spirit back to God, asking him to cleanse our hearts and make them new. (p. 68)

Is this something you've done? If not, take a few moments to pray the prayer below. (If you have done this before, take the time to affirm it.)

I surrender my life entirely to you, Christ.
I renounce all my sin.
I forsake all idols I've turned to for the life only you can give.

> I turn to you and give you my whole being, body, soul, and spirit.
> Cleanse me and make my heart new.

Until we embrace that amazing truth, we will find it really hard to make decisions, because we can't trust what our hearts are saying. We'll have to be motivated by external pressure since we can't be motivated by our heart. In fact, we won't find our calling, our places in God's kingdom, because they are written on our hearts' desires. We'll have a really hard time hearing God's voice in a deeply intimate way, because God speaks to us in our hearts. We'll live under guilt and shame for all sorts of evil thoughts and desires that the Enemy has convinced us were ours. God will seem aloof. Worship and prayer will feel like chores.

Does this describe your life?

> *Yes . . . now it does. (Craig)*

Of course, I just described the life most Christians feel doomed to live.

Now listen to Jesus:

> Each tree is recognized by its own fruit. People do not pick figs from thorn bushes, or grapes from briars. *The good man brings good things out of the good stored up in his heart*, and the evil man brings evil things out of the evil stored up in his heart. (Luke 6:44–45, emphasis added)

Later, explaining the parable of the sower and the seed, Jesus says,

> The seed on good soil stands for those *with a noble and good heart*, who hear the word, retain it, and by persevering produce a crop. (Luke 8:15, emphasis added)

Jesus himself teaches that at least for somebody, the heart can be good and even noble. That somebody is you, if you are his. God kept his promise. Our hearts have been circumcised to God. We have new hearts. Do you know what this means? Your heart is good. Let that sink in for a moment. Your heart is *good*.

What would happen if you believed it, if you came to the place where you *knew* it was true? Your life would never be the same. My friend Lynn got it, and that's when she exclaimed, "If we believed that . . . we could do *anything*. We would follow him *anywhere*!" (pp. 69–70)

Whoa! Have you ever thought of your heart being good? *Good* good? How have you or others viewed your heart? Do you find yourself hesitant to believe this reality? "Your heart is good." Let that sink in for a moment. "Your heart is *good*."

Until recently, no. I'd heard and been trained that my heart was wicked, depraved, dark, untrustworthy, stained, tainted, and forever sinful (until heaven). As for the hearts of others . . . theirs were always a little worse than mine.

What's interesting to me is that it has actually been pretty easy to believe this if you believe what God's Word says about the new covenant and the work of Christ. It's incredibly true! (Craig)

Exactly. It would change our lives. It would change the face of Christianity. This is the lost message of the gospel, lost at least to a great many people. Small wonder. This is the *last* thing the Enemy wants the world to know. It would change everything. Those of you who've gotten your hearts back know exactly what I mean. It's freedom. It's life. (p. 70)

And so, where is your heart as you end this chapter? Can you put into a sentence or two what God has said to you through this chapter?

What was the most stirring idea in this chapter for you?

What questions or desires do you want to take to God?

Or why don't you just run around the house, rejoicing? Put on some great music, and celebrate!

CHAPTER FIVE

THE GLORY HIDDEN IN YOUR HEART

The LORD their God will save them on that day
  as the flock of his people.
They will sparkle in his land
    like jewels in a crown.
How attractive and beautiful they will be!

—ZECHARIAH (9:16—17)

Those who look to him are radiant;
    their faces are never covered with shame.

—KING DAVID (PS. 34:5)

HEART MONITOR

Describe your heart toward God right now. Would postponing this chapter simply to reflect upon, pray, and enjoy God seem like a distraction, or might it be the very thing most meaningful for your heart?

So, how has the war against your heart manifested itself in your life recently? Are you beginning to see the assaults more clearly now?

What thoughts have you begun to entertain about your crucial role in God's plan?

A FIRST REACTION

What was the effect of this chapter upon you? Write out your impressions: any new or challenging thoughts, emotions, or stirrings in your heart, or even perhaps something you intend to do.

A MYTHIC PARABLE

"Have you no other daughters?" "No," said the man. "There is a little stunted kitchen wench which my late wife left behind her, but she cannot be the bride." The King's son said he was to send her up to him; but the step-mother answered, "Oh no, she is much too dirty, she cannot show herself!" But he absolutely insisted on it, and Cinderella had to be called. She first washed her hands and face clean, and then went and bowed down before the King's son, who gave her the golden slipper. Then she seated herself on a stool, drew her foot out of the heavy wooden shoe, and put it into the slipper, which fit like a glove. And when she rose up and the King's son looked at her face, he recognized the beautiful maiden who had danced with him and cried, "This is the true bride!" The step-mother and two sisters were horrified and became pale with rage; he, however, took Cinderella on his horse and rode away with her. (pp. 71–72)

What does the story stir in you? Does it open up some aspect of the Christian life to you . . . or some aspect of your life?

❧ THE BIG IDEAS

FIRST, there is a glory hidden in your heart. God endowed you with a glory when he created you, a glory so deep and mythic that all creation pales in comparison. A glory unique to you, like your fingerprints are unique to you, like the way you laugh is unique to you. Somewhere down deep inside we've been looking for that glory ever since.

SECOND, we are under a spell. We are alert and oriented times zero. We have no idea who we really are. Whatever glory was bestowed, whatever glory is being restored, we thought this whole Christian thing was about . . . something else. Trying not to sin. Going to church. Being nice. Jesus says it is about healing your heart, setting it free, restoring your glory. A religious fog has tried to veil all that, put us under some sort of spell or amnesia, to keep us from coming alive.

THIRD, you must embrace your glory. You are going to need your whole heart in all its glory for this Story you've fallen into. We know that we are not what we were meant to be. Most of us spend our energy trying to hide that fact, through all the veils we put on and the false selves we create. Far better to spend our energy trying to recover the image of God and unveil it for his glory.

Big Idea 1: WE HAVE A GLORY

I love this part of the [Cinderella] story—to see the heroine unveiled in all her glory. To have her, *finally*, rise up to her full height. Mocked, hated, laughed at, spit upon— Cinderella is the one the slipper fits; she's the one the prince is in love with; *she's* the true bride. Just as we are. We, the ransomed church, are the bride of the King's Son, are we not? "Come, I will show you the bride, the wife of the Lamb" (Rev. 21:9). We've been chosen by him. We are the object of his love. "You have stolen my heart with one glance of your eyes" (Song 4:9). This fairy tale is *true*. I love it that in this passage from the original "Cinderella," the king's son *insisted* she come out of hiding. Though her family would keep her in the cellar, he'll have none of that. Come out. You are mine now. Let your light shine before men. No more hiding. (pp. 71–72)

Do you have a sense that there's more to you than most people realize? Try to put that into words. What would it take for you to leave the cellar and live the life you could?

Is this a new thought, that the life you're living now isn't the full life Christ has in mind for you?

Not new, but this time around it seems to have a different spin. In the past the thought that I may not be living the full life Christ offers me has produced shame and condemnation that I either don't have what it takes as a Christian (I am probably lacking a real love of God, or the true commitment to obedience, or some new crisis experience with God), or God is holding out on me. For some reason he chooses not to give me the full portion. Now, I'm beginning to own my need and desire for more and am captured by the promise and availability of the offer. In other words, I'm after it. (Craig)

God's heart toward you is one of fierce love. He's coming for you, insisting you come out of the shadows, out of hiding. Has anyone come after you like that, ever?

Cinderella was called a "kitchen wench." What name or label has been put on you? Isn't there something below the wound and its message that says it isn't true? What name would you love to have put upon you?

Still, if I'm honest, I appreciate the story . . . from a distance. The thought of me being called out of hiding is unnerving. I don't think I want to be seen . . .

You probably can't imagine there being a glory to your life, let alone one that the enemy fears. But remember—things are not what they seem. We are not what we seem. You probably believed that your heart was bad too. I pray that fog of poison gas from the pit of hell is fading away in the wind of God's truth. And there is more. Not only does Christ say to you that your heart is good, he invites you now out of the shadows to unveil your glory. You have a role you never dreamed of having. (pp. 72–73)

Do you, too, share an apprehension in being "seen"? What fears do you have about being unveiled and living in your glory?

Much to everyone's surprise, Peter is unveiled at Pentecost with quite a sermon that brings three thousand converts into the church. This from the man who denied

Christ, three times, in his hour of need. Peter's buddies had to have been thinking, *Whoa, where did* that *come from*? And of course, Jesus himself, the carpenter's son, is unveiled on the Mount of Transfiguration for who he really is—the King of glory. (p. 73)

MORE CLARITY

One real obstacle to our being unveiled is the rarely spoken expectation or pressure to *remain* the same. Put into words, it might go like this: "We like you just the way you are," or "Don't ever change." Sometimes a personal change disrupts your social/relational interactions, and you may even be scorned or belittled by friends. As you have moved in the direction of your glory, have you begun to sense the pressure to remain the same? To what extent is this pressure a reality for you? How will you handle it?

The day has come and the Morning Star has risen, never to set again. This unveiling, this coming into your glory, this is inevitable for the ransomed heart. If you'll recall, Moses put a veil over his face. That, too, was a picture of a deeper reality. We all do that. We have all veiled our glory, or someone has veiled it for us. Usually, some combination of both. But the time has come to set all veils aside. (p. 74)

Whoa—"this coming into your glory, this is inevitable for the ransomed heart"! What does the inevitability of your being unveiled stir in you? What part do you play in this process?

At this very moment I want it so badly I can taste it! Do it, God! Bring it on! I'm so tired of living on four cylinders, believing you designed me for eight. This cellar is dank, dim, and small, and I'm tired of the older sisters griping. Give me the slipper... I know it fits. (Craig)

Now if the ministry that brought death, which was engraved in letters on stone, came with glory, so that the Israelites could not look steadily at the face of Moses because of its glory, fading though it was, will not the ministry of the Spirit be even more glorious? . . . Therefore, since we have such a hope, we are very bold. We are not like Moses, who would put a veil over his face to keep the Israelites from gazing at it while the radiance was fading away . . . And we, who with unveiled faces all reflect the Lord's glory, are being transformed into his likeness with ever-increasing glory, which comes from the Lord, who is the Spirit. (2 Cor. 3:7–8, 12–13, 18)

We are in the process of being unveiled. We were created to reflect God's glory, born to bear his image, and he ransomed us to reflect that glory again. Every heart was given a mythic glory, and that glory is being *restored*. Remember the mission of Christ: "I have come to give you back your heart and set you free." For as Saint Irenaeus said, "The glory of God is man fully alive." Certainly, you don't think the opposite is true. How do we bring God glory when we are sulking around in the cellar, weighed down by shame and guilt, hiding our light under a bushel? Our destiny is to come fully alive. To live with ever-*increasing* glory. This is the Third Eternal Truth every good myth has been trying to get across to us: *your heart bears a glory, and your glory is needed* . . . now. This is our desperate hour. (pp. 74–75)

Can you see this process of ever-increasing glory unfolding in your life? Could this be the beginning of a season of longed-for transformation?

Put into words a prayer for this process in your life.

In an attempt to explain the biblical doctrine of sin, we've let something else creep in. You'll hear it come up almost automatically whenever Christians talk about themselves. "I'm just a sinner, saved by grace." "I'm just clothes for God to put on." "There sure isn't any good thing in me." It's so common this mind-set, this idea that we are no-good wretches, ready to sin at a moment's notice, incapable of goodness, and certainly far from any glory.

It's also unbiblical.

The passage people think they are referring to is Romans 7:18, where Paul says, "For I know that in me (that is, in my flesh,) dwelleth no good thing" (KJV). Notice the distinction he makes. He does *not* say, "There is nothing good in me. Period." What he says is that "*in my flesh* dwelleth no good thing." The flesh is the old nature, the old life, crucified with Christ. The flesh is the very thing God removed from our hearts when he circumcised them by his Spirit. In Galatians Paul goes on to explain, "Those who belong to Christ Jesus have crucified the sinful nature [the flesh] with its passions and desires" (5:24). He does *not* say, "I am incapable of good." He says, "*In my flesh* dwelleth no good thing." In fact, just a few moments later, what he discovers is that "the law of the Spirit of life in Christ Jesus has set me free from the law of sin and death" (Rom. 8:2 NKJV). (pp. 75–76)

It's so plain and clear, yet we've missed it. Does what Paul describes in Romans 8:2 sound decisive and permanent?

In a column, write out the fruits of the flesh that have manifested themselves in your life:

_____

_____

_____

_____

According to Galatians 5:24, what has happened to your flesh and everything represented on your list?

So, why do so many lives reflect the fruit of the flesh instead of the Spirit?

Yes, we still battle with sin. *Yes*, we still have to crucify our flesh on a daily basis. "For if you live according to the flesh you will die; but if by the Spirit you put to death the deeds of the [sinful nature], you will live" (Rom. 8:13 NKJV). We have to *choose* to live from the new heart, and our old nature doesn't go down without a fight. I'll say more about that later. For now the question on the table is: Does the Bible teach that Christians are nothing but sinners—that there is nothing good in us? The answer is *no!* You have a new heart. Your heart is good. That sinful nature you battle *is not who you are.* Twice, in the famous chapter of Romans 7, where Paul presents a first-person angst about our battle against sin, he says, "But this is not my true nature. This is not my heart." (p. 76)

Respond/react to this paragraph. What does this stir up in you?

Freedom! It always seemed deep inside that Christ's work was more significant than I had personally experienced. I knew forgiveness, but I sensed that Christ had done more for me . . . something inside had changed . . . that, despite all evidence to the contrary, I was a new creature and something had died. It's true. (Craig)

As it is, *it is no longer I myself* who do it, but it is sin living in me. I know that nothing good lives in me, that is, in my sinful nature . . . Now if I do what I do not want to do, *it is no longer I* who do it, but it is sin living in me that does it . . . For in my inner being I delight in God's law. (vv. 17–18, 20, 22, emphasis added)

Paul is making a crucial distinction: *This is not me; this is not my true heart.* Listen to how he talks about himself in other places. He opens every letter by introducing himself as "Paul, an apostle." Not as a sinner, but as an apostle, writing to "the saints." Dump the religiosity; think about this *mythically.* Paul, appointed as a Great One in the kingdom, writing other Great Allies of the kingdom. How bold of him. There is no false humility, no groveling. He says,

Surely you have heard about the . . . grace that was given to me for you, that is, the mystery made known to me by revelation, as I have already written briefly. In reading this, then, you will be able to understand my insight into the mystery of Christ, which was not made known to men in other generations as it has now been revealed [to me]. (Eph. 3:2–5)

Paul is unashamed to say that he knows things no man before him knew. He even assumes they've heard about him, the mysteries revealed to him. That is part of his glory. His humility comes through clearly, in that he quickly admits that it's all been a gift, and in fact, a gift given to him *for others.*

And listen to the way he talks about us: "You shine like stars in the universe as you hold out the word of life" (Phil. 2:15–16) . . . All this groveling and self-deprecation done by Christians is usually shame masquerading as humility. Shame says, "I'm nothing to look at. I'm not capable of goodness." Humility says, "I bear a glory for sure, but it is a *reflected* glory. A grace given to me." Your story does not begin with sin. It begins with a glory bestowed upon you by God. It does not start in Genesis 3; it starts in Genesis 1. First things first, as they say. (pp. 76–77)

What words have you heard from the shame-based "You're nothing but a worm" tape that's played in your head? (It's probably similar to the message that comes with our wounds.)

"You simply do not have what it takes. Look at you; you have nothing to offer. You live in a fantasy world of make-believe to think that you—you—could play a significant role for God. But hey, go ahead, try to fool the others—but you can't fool me . . . or yourself. You know it's true!" (Craig)

Certainly, you will admit that God is glorious. Is there anyone more kind? Is there anyone more creative? Is there anyone more valiant? Is there anyone more true? Is there anyone more daring? Is there anyone more beautiful? Is there anyone more wise? Is there anyone more generous? You are his offspring. His child. His reflection. His likeness. You bear *his* image. Do remember that though he made the heavens and the earth in all their glory, the desert and the open sea, the meadow and the Milky Way, and said, "It is good," it was only *after* he made you that he said, "It is *very* good" (Gen. 1:31). Think of it: your original glory was greater than anything that's ever taken your breath away in nature.

> As for the saints who are in the land,
>> they are the glorious ones in whom is all my delight. (Ps. 16:3)

God endowed you with a glory when he created you, a glory so deep and mythic that all creation pales in comparison. A glory unique to you, just as your fingerprints are unique to you, just as the way you laugh is unique to you. Somewhere down deep inside we've been looking for that glory ever since. A man wants to know that he is truly a man, that he could be brave; he longs to know that he is a warrior; and all his life he wonders, "Have I got what it takes?" A woman wants to know that she is truly a woman, that she is beautiful; she longs to know she is captivating; and all her life she wonders, "Do I have a beauty to offer?" (pp. 77–78)

What emotion do you feel immediately after reading this paragraph? What do you want to do right now, at this moment, after reading this?

> I want to scream "Yes!" and fall on my knees, thanking God. And I want to charge the enemy of my heart. (Craig)

When you take a second glance in the mirror, when you pause to look again at a photograph, you are looking for a glory you know you were meant to have, if only because you know you long to have it. You remember faintly that you were once more than what you have become. Your story didn't start with sin, and thank God, it does not end with sin. It ends with glory restored: "Those he justified, he also glorified" (Rom. 8:30). And "in the meantime," you have *been* transformed, and you are *being* transformed. You've been given a new heart. Now God is restoring your glory. He is bringing you fully alive. Because the glory of God is you fully alive. (pp. 78–79)

What would you love to have said about you? Take the time to go through old photos. Remember the desires and dreams you had for yourself as a youngster . . . what would you have loved to accomplish, to be?

In the presence of Christ I love to hear, "Well done, Craig! You're everything I hoped you would be." And then from others, "Because of the power and weight of your life, I, too, have to live a full life." I'd love to be a leader in the development of redemptive communities/churches that are powerfully living out the gospel. (Craig)

Big Idea 2: WE ARE UNDER A SPELL

"Well then, if this is all true, how come I don't see it?" Precisely. Exactly. Now we are reaching my point. The fact that you do not see your good heart and your glory is only proof of how effective the assault has been. We don't see ourselves clearly. Have you forgotten your fairy tales? (p. 79)

Is that you—you don't see it? And why might that be?

We are under a spell. We are alert and oriented times zero. We have no idea who we really are. Whatever glory was bestowed, whatever glory is being restored, we thought this whole Christian thing was about . . . something else. Trying not to sin. Going to church. Being nice. Jesus says it is about healing your heart, setting it free, restoring your glory. A religious fog has tried to veil all that, put us under some sort of spell or amnesia, to keep us from coming alive. Pascal said, "It is a monstrous thing . . . an incomprehensible enchantment, and a supernatural slumber." And Paul said, It is time to take that veil away. (p. 80)

Are you beginning to awaken from a slumber, the spell? Look into the mirror now, and then again over the next week. Look into your eyes, closely: are you beginning to see something new?

What's been taken, stolen, prevented in your life? How has the Enemy kept you enchanted—under a veil all these years?

Taking every advantage he could through wounds, fear, my sin, and spiritual passivity, he has filled a cavern with the loot he has stolen: vacations and special moments with my wife and daughters, closer relationships with my siblings and extended family, memories, focus and discipline, time, opportunities for adventure and beauty, impact upon others, clarity and courage.

The enemy has used my wounds and broken places as a foothold from which to lie to, cheat, deceive, and rob me. The gig's up. (Craig)

Whenever anyone turns to the Lord, the veil is taken away. Now the Lord is the Spirit, and where the Spirit of the Lord is, there is freedom. And we, who with unveiled faces all reflect the Lord's glory, are being transformed into his likeness with ever-increasing glory, which comes from the Lord, who is the Spirit. (2 Cor. 3:16–18)

A veil removed, bringing freedom, transformation, glory. Do you see it? I am not making this up—though I have been accused of making the gospel better than it is. The charge is laughable. Could anyone be more generous than God? Could any of us come up with a story that beats the one God has come up with? (pp. 80–81)

In these first five chapters, what are you beginning to believe about yourself that is true and new? Write these things down and keep them in an accessible spot to recall during the assaults against what's true about you.

Big Idea 3: YOU MUST EMBRACE YOUR GLORY

You are going to need your whole heart in all its glory for this Story you've fallen into . . . So, who did God mean when he meant you? We at least know this: we know that we are not what we were meant to be. Most of us spend our energy trying to hide that fact, through all the veils we put on and the false selves we create . . . Far better to spend our energy trying to recover the image of God and unveil it for his glory. (pp. 82–83)

What false self have you substituted for your true glory?

My false self presents a freedom and "life," a Christian "maturity" unaffected by any circumstances or difficulties. I'm a nice guy, witty, insightful, easygoing, caring, and incredibly resilient. It all looks deeply authentic and godly, but it's all so very shallow and untrue. (Craig)

One means that will help us is any story that helps us see with the eyes of the heart. Which brings us back to myth. Poet David Whyte says, "Myths reveal to us what we are capable of." Clyde Kilby offers this image: "Myth is a lane down which we walk in order to repossess our soul." Wow! Wouldn't you love to repossess your soul? To live with an unmasked, unveiled glory that reflects the glory of the Lord? That's worth fighting for. (p. 83)

Whom were you meant to be?

What would rising up and fighting for your glory look like?

The Bible is filled with characters . . . Abraham is a character; so is his wife, Sarah. King David is a character. The disciples of Jesus are all characters. Take James and John, for instance, "the sons of Zebedee." You might remember them as the ones who cornered Jesus to angle for the choice seats at his right and left hands in the kingdom. Or the time they wanted to call down fire from heaven to destroy a village that wouldn't offer Jesus a place for the night. Their buddies called them idiots; Jesus called them the Sons of Thunder (Mark 3:17). He sees who they *really* are. It's their mythic name, their true identity. They look like fishermen out of work; they are actually the Sons of Thunder.

There are stories that you've loved, there are characters that you've resonated with down deep inside, maybe even dreamed that you could be. Do you know why? Deep is calling unto deep. They spoke to you—they speak even now—because they contain some hint or glimpse into your true self. (pp. 83–84)

What characters have you resonated with?

Read John's story of his "personal myth" in the section "What Our Myths Reveal" on pages 84–86.

Have you ever asked God, "God, who am I?" "What do you think of me?" "What's my real name?" Set aside several hours, or better yet, a day. Design it to find and converse with God regarding these questions. What did you hear?

God took me into the truth of the mythic name through the doorway of my own heart and my desires. I was trapped; there was no denying now that it was God who spoke that morning. I was forced to wrestle with the fact that what he spoke was true. Over the past year I have needed that mythic name and all the strength and courage it offers. The battle has been ugly, and there are many hearts to free. The Accuser laughs and mocks and throws everything he can: "You are making this up. You are a weak little man." *Ego numquam pronunciare mendacium, sed ego sum homo indomitus.* I never tell lies, but I am a savage. (p. 86)

Have you found the Accuser laughing at and mocking you, suggesting that you are making this up? Does he say, "You are a weak little man"? What has the attack on your true identity looked like? How has it come to you?

If the Accuser, the Thief, will throw everything and anything at you to keep you from knowing who you truly are and moving into your glory, what must you do to counter it?

I have to keep what's true about me before me. My fellowship reminds me of what's true; so does my journal—in it I record the personal words and lessons God has given me. (Craig)

Our deepest fear is not that we are inadequate. *Our deepest fear is that we are powerful beyond measure.* It is our light, not our darkness, that most frightens us. We ask ourselves, "Who am I to be brilliant, gorgeous, talented and fabulous?" Actually, who are you not to be? You are a child of God. Your playing small doesn't serve the world. There's nothing enlightened about shrinking so that other people won't feel insecure around you. We were born to manifest the glory of God that is within us . . . And as we let our own light shine, we unconsciously give other people permission to do the same. As we are liberated from our own fear, our presence automatically liberates others. (Nelson Mandela, emphasis added) (p. 87)

It almost seems hard to believe that our deeper fear is that we are powerful beyond measure. Do you see this fear in your life? Can you relate to this? Is that, indeed, your deepest fear? Why is it present, where has it come from?

The deeper reason we fear our own glory is because once we let others see it, they will have seen the truest us, and that is nakedness indeed. We can repent of our sin. We can work on our "issues." But there is nothing to be "done" about our glory. It's so naked. It's just there—the truest us. It is an awkward thing to shimmer when everyone else around you is not, to walk in your glory with an unveiled face when everyone else is veiling his. For a woman to be truly feminine and beautiful is to invite suspicion, jealousy, misunderstanding. A friend confided in me, "When you walk into a room, every woman looks at you to see—are you prettier than they are? Are you a threat?" (pp. 87–88)

What do you think of this explanation for our fear of our glory? Do you see it in your life?

And that is why living from your glory is the only loving thing to do. You cannot love another person from a false self. You cannot love another while you are still hiding . . . You cannot love another unless you offer her your heart. It takes courage to live from your heart . . .

. . . Finally, our deepest fear of all . . . we will need to live from it. To admit we do have a new heart and a glory from God, to begin to let it be unveiled and embrace it as true—that means the next thing God will do is ask us to live from it. Come out of the boat. Take the throne. Be what he meant us to be. And that feels risky . . . really risky. But it is also exciting. It is coming fully alive. As my friend Morgan declared, "It's a risk worth taking." (p. 88)

And so, where is your heart as you end this chapter? Can you put into a sentence or two what God has said to you through this chapter?

What was the most stirring idea in this chapter for you?

What questions or desires do you want to take to God?

PART THREE

THE FOUR STREAMS

Did you feel the darkness tremble?
When all the saints joined in one song
And all the streams flow as one river
To wash away our brokenness.

—MARTIN SMITH,
"DID YOU FEEL THE MOUNTAINS TREMBLE?"

From Eden a river flowed to water the park, which on
leaving the park branched into four streams.

—GEN. 2:10 (MOFFATT)

In the Garden known as Eden there was a spring. Issuing from the depths of the earth, this fount became the headwaters of a mighty river, which in turn parted into four great streams. Saint Bonaventure saw in that a foreshadowing, a mythic symbol of "an ever-flowing fountain," as he called it, "that becomes a great and living river with four channels to water the garden of the entire Church." I think if you will look again at the ways in which Christ ransoms people, the *means* by which he makes a man or a woman come fully alive, you'll find he offers his life to us through Four Streams. Those streams are Discipleship, Counseling, Healing, and Warfare.

The *terms* might sound familiar; but for so many of us they are familiar in the way that we've heard Saturn has rings around it or that Antarctica is a frozen continent. Our actual *experience* of the Four Streams is not what it could be . . . if it were, we would be "the glorious ones" by now (Ps. 16:3). It will help to think of them as Walking with God, Receiving His Intimate Counsel, Deep Restoration, and Spiritual Warfare.

Long have these streams been separated. I imagine we've sipped from only one or two. Now is the time for them to flow together again. That is how our glory is restored, how we find the life Christ offers, how we live in his Story. To discover for yourself that the glory of God *is* man fully alive, you must drink deeply from the Four Streams that Christ sends to you. (pp. 89–90)

CHAPTER SIX

WALKING WITH GOD

Narrow the road that leads to life, and only a few find it.
—JESUS (MATT. 7:14)

You have made known to me the path of life.
—KING DAVID (PS. 16:11)

HEART MONITOR

Has your pace of going through this guidebook given you time to reflect, perhaps journal and converse with God about all you are learning and pondering? Would taking a quiet walk, or enjoying some music, art, or even a rich conversation with an old friend help you prepare for this chapter?

Has the knowledge that you have a new heart, a *good* heart, moved from your head into how you've lived this week? How you have related to God and others? Jot down your thoughts.

As you embrace this reality more and more, you'll begin to note that Christians you interface with also have good hearts, whether or not they realize it or live from it. How does this impact the way you relate to your Christian friends, even the annoying ones?

When you believe that your heart is good, you become much more dangerous to the kingdom of darkness. In what ways has your heart been assaulted this week? Are you beginning to discern and catch the various ways you can lose heart?

As you continue to think of your crucial role . . . what negative voices do you hear challenging such a place in God's plan? What assaults your understanding of how God wants to use you in the Larger Story?

FIRST REACTION

What was the effect of this chapter upon you? Write out your impressions: any new or challenging thoughts, emotions or stirrings in your heart, or even perhaps something you intend to do.

A MYTHIC PARABLE

After the Road had run down some way, and had left Bree-hill standing tall and brown behind, they came on a narrow track that led off towards the North. "This is where we leave the open road and take to cover," said Strider.

"Not a 'short cut' I hope," said Pippin. "Our last short cut through woods nearly ended in disaster."

"Ah, but you had not got me with you then," laughed Strider. "My cuts, short or long, don't go wrong." He took a look up and down the Road. No one was in sight; and he led the way quickly down towards the wooded valley . . .

Strider guided them confidently among the many crossing paths, although left to themselves they would soon have been at a loss. He was taking a wandering course with many turns and doublings, to put off any pursuit . . . Whether because of Strider's skill or for some other reason, they saw no sign and heard no sound of any other living thing all that day . . .

They had not gone far on the fifth day when they left the last straggling pools and reed beds of the marshes behind them. The land before them began steadily to rise again. Away in the distance eastward they could now see a line of hills. The highest of them was at the right of the line and a little separated from the others. It had a conical top, slightly flattened at the summit. "That is Weathertop," said Strider . . .

They stood for a while silent on the hilltop, near its southern edge. In that lonely place Frodo for the first time fully realized his homelessness and danger. He wished bitterly that his fortune had left him in the quiet and beloved Shire. He stared down at the hateful Road, leading back westward—to his home. Suddenly he was aware that two black specks were moving slowly along it, going westward; and looking again he saw that three others were creeping eastward to meet them. He gave a cry and clutched Strider's arm. "Look," he said, pointing downwards. At once Strider flung himself on the ground behind the ruined circle, pulling Frodo down beside him. Merry threw himself alongside.

Slowly they crawled up to the edge of the ring again, and peered through a cleft between two jagged stones. The light was no longer bright, for the clear morning had faded . . . neither Frodo nor Merry could make out their shapes for certain; yet something told them that there, far below, were Black Riders assembling on the Road beyond the foot of the hill. "Yes," said Strider, whose keener sight left him in no doubt. "The enemy is here!" (J. R. R. Tolkien, *The Fellowship of the Ring*) (pp. 91–92)

What does the story stir in you? Does it open up some aspect of the Christian life to you . . . or some aspect of your life?

❋ THE BIG IDEAS

FIRST, we need a Guide. If you're not pursuing a dangerous quest with your life, well, then, you don't need a Guide. Given the reality of the war we're engaged in and the various assaults on our hearts, we truly need a Guide.

SECOND, discipleship is learning to walk with God. Only by walking with God can we hope to find the path that leads to life. *That* is what it means to be a disciple.

THIRD, walking with God involves wisdom.

FOURTH, walking with God involves revelation. Wisdom is crucial. But wisdom is not enough.

Big Idea 1: WE NEED A GUIDE

If you're not pursuing a dangerous quest with your life, well, then, you don't need a Guide. If you haven't found yourself in the midst of a ferocious war, then you won't need a seasoned Captain. If you've settled in your mind to live as though this is a fairly neutral world and you are simply trying to live your life as best you can, then you can probably get by with the Christianity of tips and techniques. Maybe. I'll give you about a fifty-fifty chance. But if you intend to live in the Story that God is telling, and if you want the life he offers, then you are going to need more than a handful of principles, however noble they may be. There are too many twists and turns in the road ahead, too many ambushes waiting only God knows where, too much at stake. You cannot possibly prepare yourself for every situation. Narrow is the way, said Jesus. How shall we be sure to find it? We need God intimately, and we need him desperately. (p. 95)

What's at stake? What danger do you face? What quest are you on? Does the life you are living *really* require a Guide, or can you pretty much make it on your own? Explain.

I want to be on a quest that requires God. I found it easy to live a life that requires only a few biblical principles and techniques. In some ways it seems easier just to get up and check off my list of do's and don'ts for the day and call that following God. But more and more it's less appealing. There's no clear-cut "how-to" for the quest God has me on.

At this time my quest involves creating a new church, a redemptive community, that is unlike any I've been involved in. It would be much safer and might turn out to be more "successful" if I followed the traditional paradigm I've lived in for twenty-five years as a pastor. But for years the desire for a new wineskin has burned in my soul. My best ideas, thinking, and convictions about church could all end up failing, and failing on this level seems like a final judgment on my life, terrifying—yet very much worth the risk. (Craig)

What fears or concerns do you have about walking with God? Will he even want to walk with you? Do you wonder if you'll be able to keep up, or will you slow him down? Or on a deeper level, do you have a reluctance to follow him because you want to retain control of your life? What would it take to follow, to trust his leading? Where are some of the difficult places God leads us?

First off, walking with Christ and enjoying an intimate relationship with him is my defining desire. I know that's sure. I know he's good and that his plans for me are for good. I also know he's wild and mysterious at times. His ways don't always match my preferences, soooo, yeah, I have "fears," "concerns," or hesitations. There are those little voices that can get pretty loud, suggesting, "You can't really trust him on this one!" or "Just live your life directed by your preferences— don't check in with God. If you're really blowing it, he'll let you know. You're free, after all, right?" Sadly, I listen to those voices at times. Control can be huge for me. Yuck, I hate admitting that.

Some of the difficult places God leads me are: into situations that require more of me as a man than I believe I have to offer (particularly as a husband and pastor); into forgiving someone who has assaulted me; into genuine humility; into opening doors to exercise gifts and a calling I believe I have but am still young in; into listening to someone whom, on the surface, I find horribly annoying . . . I could go on for quite a while. (Craig)

Do you believe that God speaks to all of us or that he has favorites to whom he may speak more intimately/often? Has God's "speaking" to you over the years changed in some ways? In what ways?

"You have made known to me the path of life," David said (Ps. 16:11). Yes—that's it. In all the ins and outs of this thing we call living, there is one narrow path to life, and we need help finding it. (p. 95)

Big Idea 2: DISCIPLESHIP IS LEARNING TO WALK WITH GOD

On the other hand, there is what we have come to accept as discipleship. A friend of mine recently handed me a program from a large and successful church somewhere in the Midwest. It's a rather exemplary model of what the idea has fallen to. Their plan for discipleship involves, first, becoming a member of this particular church. Then they encourage you to take a course on doctrine. Be "faithful" in attending both the Sunday morning service and a small group fellowship. Complete a special course on Christian growth. Live a life that demonstrates clear evidence of spiritual growth. Complete a class on evangelism. Consistently look for opportunities to evangelize. Complete a course on finances, one on marriage, and another on parenting (provided that you are married or a parent). Complete a leadership training course, a hermeneutics course, a course on spiritual gifts, and another on biblical counseling. Participate in missions. Carry a significant local church ministry "load."

. . . No doubt a great deal of helpful information is passed on . . . But let me ask you: A program like this—does it teach a person how to apply principles, or how to walk with God? They are not the same thing. (pp. 95–96)

In your words, describe the difference between learning principles about God and learning how to walk with God. Which has been the focus of your discipleship experiences?

We forfeit that birthright when we take folks through a discipleship program whereby they master any number of Christian precepts and miss the most important thing of all, the very thing for which we were created: intimacy with God. There are, after all, those troubling words Jesus spoke to those who were doing all the "right" things: "Then I will tell them plainly, 'I never knew you'" (Matt. 7:23). Knowing God. That's the point.

. . . After all—aren't we "followers of Christ"? Then by all means, let's actually *follow* him. Not ideas about him. Not just his principles. Him. (pp. 96–97)

In your discipleship experiences, how was intimacy with God defined/presented/ understood? As a result, did you enjoy the intimacy you sought?

In my early years—gosh, I sound old—when I first accepted Christ, the group I was being discipled by understood intimacy as an abiding personal, conversational relationship. Unfortunately, much of it was dependent upon regular crisis experiences with God . . . and those became harder and harder to conjure up. In seminary and for years following, intimacy wasn't really referred to; it simply wasn't a concept embraced. The ability to properly exegete, expositionally preach, and apply the Word of God was what was required of me to stem the tide of heresy of every kind. And there were many, many heresies to police. I thank God for his Word and for most of what I've learned, but I'm finding again the personal abiding and heartfelt communion that the Word presents (without the kookiness) . . . and I love it! (Craig)

You might recall the old proverb: "Give a man a fish and you feed him for a day; teach a man to fish and you feed him for a lifetime." The same holds true here. Teach a man a rule and you help him solve a problem; teach a man to walk with God and you help him solve the rest of his life. Truth be told, you couldn't master enough principles to see you safely through this Story. There are too many surprises, ambiguities, exceptions to the rule. Things are hard at work—is it time to make a move? What has God called you to do with your life? Things are hard at home—is this just a phase your son is going through, or should you be more concerned? You can't seem to shake this depression—is it medical or something darker? What does the future hold for you—and how should you respond? (pp. 96–97)

Think of a recent decision in which you were not really sure what direction to take. Did you take it to God? If not, why not? If so, what was his reply?

Only by walking with God can we hope to find the path that leads to life. *That* is what it means to be a disciple. (p. 97)

Big Idea 3: WALKING WITH GOD INVOLVES WISDOM

A personal walk with God comes to us through wisdom and revelation. You will soon discover that we need both.

For a moment the King's grief and anger were so great that he could not speak. Then he said: "Come, friends. We must go up the river and find the villains who have done this, with all the speed we may. I will not leave one of them alive." "Sire, with a good will," said Jewel. But Roonwit said, "Sire, be wary in your just wrath. There are strange doings on foot. If there should be rebels in arms further up the valley, we three are too few to meet them. If it would please you to wait while . . ." "I will not wait the tenth part of a second," said the King. "But while Jewel and I go forward, do you gallop as hard as you may to Cair Paravel . . . we must go on and take the adventure that comes to us. It is the only thing left for us to do, Sire," said the Unicorn. He did not see at the moment how foolish it was for two of them to go on alone; nor did the King. They were too angry to think clearly. But much evil came of their rashness in the end. (C. S. Lewis, *The Last Battle*)

King Tirian of Narnia has a good heart. But he also has an unwise heart—an untrained heart. I'd say that's true for most of us. Our heart has been made good by the work of Christ, but we haven't learned how to live from it. Young and naive it remains. It's as though we've been handed a golden harp or a shining sword. Even the most gifted musician still has to take lessons; even the bravest of warriors must be trained. We are unfamiliar, unpracticed with the ways of the heart. This is actually a very dangerous part of the journey. Launching out with an untrained heart can bring much hurt and ruin, and afterwards we will be shamed back into the gospel of Sin Management, having concluded that our heart is bad. It isn't bad; it's just young and unwise. (pp. 97–98)

You can have a good heart and live like a moron or even worse. We cannot assume that a good heart is a wise heart. How wise, skilled, and trained is your heart?

I've had a naïve heart, lacking in wisdom and skill, untrained, constrained. I wish I knew earlier in life what I'm learning now. I think of how differently I would have responded to and loved my wife, raised my daughters, and led my church. (Craig)

There's knowledge and then there's wisdom. What's the difference? Whom in your life have you respected as a wise person? What was his or her relationship with Christ like?

When the apostles needed the help of some good men to shepherd the exploding new church, they chose men "full of the Spirit and wisdom" (Acts 6:3). The two go together; we need both. We need to walk by the inspiration of the Spirit, and we need wisdom as well. Wisdom and revelation. Early on in our journey, I think we should lean more into wisdom. It takes time to learn to walk with God in a deeply intimate way, and many challenges face us before we are accustomed to the way of the heart. We must practice our chords; we must do our drills. (p. 98)

TO CLARIFY

A starting place for those young in wisdom would be to simply begin to read and listen to the Word. A few basic questions to ask as you read would be:

What jumps off the pages? Impressions, new thoughts, a different way of living life, unease with my life, questions . . .

What am I learning about God? What is God like? What is his heart/posture for me?

What am I learning about people, about myself? What is man's posture toward God? What drives the choices we make? How would I like to live and relate to God?

What am I learning about life/reality? How does the life God desires for us differ from the life I am living?

You may want to begin your training in wisdom by beginning to read the Gospels, Proverbs, and Psalms.

Read Proverbs 1:20, 32–33, 2:9–11. How accessible is wisdom? Where does wisdom reside?

Wisdom was crying out: do not rush the field (Luke 14:31); train yourself to discern good and evil (Heb. 5:14); live as though your life is at stake, and the Enemy is waiting to outwit you (Matt. 10:16). God has given us all sorts of counsel and direction in his written Word; thank God, we have it written down in black and white. We would do well to be familiar with it, study it with all the intensity of the men who studied the maps of the Normandy coastline before they hit the beaches on D-Day. The more that wisdom enters our hearts, the more we will be able to trust our hearts in difficult situations. Notice that wisdom is not cramming our heads with principles. It is developing a discerning *heart*. What made Solomon such a sharp guy was his wise and discerning heart (1 Kings 3:9).

We don't seek wisdom because it's a good idea; we seek wisdom because we're dead if we don't. (pp. 99–100)

Practically, what will you do to continue to gain wisdom?

Big Idea 4: WALKING WITH GOD INVOLVES REVELATION

Wisdom is crucial. But wisdom is not enough. Many well-meaning evangelicals rely on it exclusively. That is why their lives remain where they are—rather short of all Christ promised. Okay—way short. Wisdom is essential . . . and insufficient.

Saul of Tarsus was headed to Damascus, "breathing out murderous threats against the Lord's disciples," with official documents granting him permission to arrest all Christians in the city and have them sent to prison (Acts 9:1–2). Now, you and I know that Jesus changed Saul's agenda rather radically before he ever reached the city—the blinding light, the voice from heaven, the total realignment of his worldview. But the believers in Damascus didn't know all this. As they wait in fear for Saul's arrival, God speaks to one of them, a man named Ananias, and tells him to go to the house where Saul is staying, lay hands on him, and pray for him. Understandably, Ananias suggests this is not such a good idea: "Lord . . . I have heard many reports about this man and all the harm he has done to your saints in Jerusalem. And he has come here with authority from the chief priests to arrest all who call on your name" (9:13–14). It's okay, God says, he's my man now. Against wisdom Ananias goes, and the greatest of all the apostles is launched.

The Bible is full of such counterintuitive direction from God. (pp. 100–101)

Can you think of other examples?

Would you counsel a father to sacrifice his only child, the only hope for the promised nation? Certainly, it wasn't wisdom that compelled a fugitive to walk back into the country where he was wanted for murder, a land where all his kin were held as slaves, march into Pharaoh's palace and demand their release. Was it reasonable to take a fortified city by marching around it blowing trumpets? What's the sense of slashing the ranks of your army from 32,000 to 300, just before battle? It was dangerous advice, indeed, to send the young maiden before her king unbidden, and even worse to send a boy against a trained mercenary. And frankly, it looked like perfect madness for Jesus to give himself up to the authorities, let himself get killed. (p. 101)

Why is it so difficult to heed counterintuitive direction? Ultimately, what is God asking from us when he directs us to do something that, to us, makes no sense? Has God led you to do counterintuitive things? Write out an example. What did he ask of you?

My wife and I recently moved from the beach in Southern California to the mountains of Colorado. In so many ways I felt like God was asking me to leave everything to follow him. I left my two daughters and our times together as family, along with lifelong, intimate friends. Why? Wasn't this the very life I'd longed to live? I will no longer have the ocean and all its mystery, life, and beauty; fog, gulls and dolphins; the sound of surf and the sunsets and reunions and fun of beach volleyball. This makes no sense—we're Southern California people! I left a ministry I "had down"— true, it required little from me, but it provided generously in pay, benefits, perks, and comfort. On and on I could go. It made no sense to us, was counterintuitive, and it was very clearly what God was asking of us. (Craig)

We still weep and deeply miss all we've left behind; and at the same time, we have never felt more in sync with God's call on our lives.

Somewhere in our hearts I think we'd all love to have a role like that, be used by God so dramatically. To find it, wisdom is just not enough—may even hold us *back* from doing the will of God. The particular foolishness of the church in the past century was Reason above all else. The result has been a faith stripped of the supernatural, the Christianity of tips and techniques. The commonsense life, which, as Oswald Chambers warned, can be the enemy of the supernatural life. Most of the ministries and churches I know make their decisions by principles and expedience. We have our morals and we have our precepts, but where is the living God? How will we hear him call us out of Ur, lead us to our own promised land, bring us through our own Calvary? Putting all our confidence in human reason was naive, and it left us in a very dangerous position. The only way out of this mess is to turn to our Guide, our Captain, to walk with God. (pp. 101–2)

Chambers said, "The common-sense life can be the enemy of the supernatural life." Does his comment frighten you or affirm you? Why?

Both. I understand that common sense can be the enemy of the supernatural. But at times common sense feels like the Divine Universal Plan from which to waver is to invite sheer destruction and shame. I'm growing here . . . slowly, but growing. (Craig)

The encouragement to include revelation in your walk: what does that elicit from you? Do you fear the mystery of it, concerned that you'll become a cult follower or a wacky TV evangelist? Do you affirm the personal dimension and intimacy of it, or perhaps fear that if you listened you wouldn't hear anything because of your sin, shame, and unworthy nature?

You betcha. It stirs some fear of becoming kooky. How many nuts have claimed to have heard God tell them to act on some half-witted idea? I've been there, done that. I threw the baby out with the bathwater, though: I swung over to the Doctrine Nazis, who know every jot and tittle of the Word but live uninviting, superficial lives, substituting clichés for a personal relationship with Christ. Some know all about God but give no indication of knowing him. Neither bandwagon appeals to me. I want the conversational, intimate relationship the Bible describes. I've enjoyed rediscovering God's wonderful involvement in my life. (Craig)

We begin by assuming that God is still speaking.

An old hymn celebrating the wonderful Scriptures has a line that goes something like this: "What more can he say, than to you he has said?" The implication being that God has said all he has to say to us in the Bible. Period. It sounds orthodox. Except that's not what the Bible says: "I have much more to say to you, more than you can now bear. But when he, the Spirit of truth, comes, he will guide you into all truth" (John 16:12–13). There's more that Jesus wants to say to you, much more, and now that his Spirit resides in your heart, the conversation can continue. Many good people never hear God speak to them personally for the simple fact that they've never been told that he *does*. But he does—generously, intimately. "He who belongs to God hears what God says" (John 8:47).

The man who enters by the gate is the shepherd of his sheep. The watchman opens the gate for him, and the sheep listen to his voice. He calls his own sheep by name and leads them out. When he has brought out all his own, he goes on ahead of them, and his sheep follow him because they know his voice . . . I am the good shepherd. (John 10:2–4, 11)

You don't just leave sheep to find their way in the world. They are famous for getting lost, attacked by wild animals, falling into some pit, and that is why they must stay close to the shepherd, follow his voice. And no shepherd could be called good unless he personally guided his flock through danger. But that is precisely what he promises to do. He *wants* to speak to you; he wants to lead you to good pasture. (pp. 102–103)

The Scripture is clear: God desires and does speak to his people. Are you gaining confidence that this is, indeed, true?

Now, it doesn't happen in an instant. Walking with God is a way of life. It's something to be learned; our ability to hear God's voice and discern his word to us grows over time. (p. 103)

When does the learning end? Are you a patient, graceful learner?

Yes, for the most part, I am a patient and graceful learner. It seems to me the goal is to walk with God today, at this moment, right now in whatever circumstances or relational difficulties I may be facing. That's very doable and ultimately leads to all the goals I used to strive and battle to achieve (under some unspoken pressure to be perfect, holy, loving, and without sin by . . . yesterday). God is changing me, in his time, from the inside out. He's patient and so am I. After all, who am I trying to please? (Craig)

Some thoughts on listening and learning how to walk with God:

1. We must *ask*.

> And we will sometimes struggle *to* hear and struggle with *what* we hear. But personally, it's worth it. I'm after the path of life—and he alone knows it. (p. 103)

What kind of things do you ask God, and when do you usually go to him with your requests?

2. Pay attention to your heart.

> When we set out to hear God's voice, we do not listen as though it will come from somewhere above us or in the room around us. It comes to us from *within*, in our heart, the dwelling place of God. Now, most of us haven't been trained in this, and it's going to take a little practice "tuning in" to all that's going on in there. And there's a lot going on in there, by the way. Many things are trying to play upon the beautiful instrument of the heart. Advertisers are constantly trying to pull on your heartstrings. So is your boss. The devil is a master at manipulating the heart. So are many people— though they wouldn't ever admit that that is what they are doing. How will you know what is compelling you? "Who can map out the various forces at play in one soul?" asked Augustine, a man who was the first to write out the story of listening to his heart. "Man is a great depth, O Lord . . . but the hairs of his head are easier by far to count than . . . the movements of his heart."
>
> This can be distressing at times. All sorts of awful things can seem to issue from your heart—anger, lust, fear, petty jealousies. If you think it's you, a reflection of what's really going on your heart, it will disable you. It could stop your journey dead in its tracks. What you've encountered is either the voice of your flesh, or an attempt of the Enemy to distress you by throwing all sorts of thoughts your way and blaming you for it. You must proceed on this assumption: your heart is good. If it seems that some foul thing is at work there, say to yourself, *Well, then—this is not my heart. My heart is good. I reject this.* Remember Paul in Romans 7? This is not me. *This is not me.* And carry on in your journey. Over time you'll grow familiar with the movements of your heart, and who is trying to influence you there. (pp. 105–6)

TO CLARIFY

God's speaking can sound like "us" because he is so intertwined with us. His desires are written in our hearts and upon our desires. Wisdom is both gained and given to us by God—this mixture is important.

Take some time now to pray. Ask God to speak. Do you hear all the distressing, distracting clutter—and yet beneath it, can you sense another voice with a different message?

3. Test what you hear.

We do the same with any counsel or word that presents itself as being from God, but contradicts what he has said to us in his written Word. We walk with wisdom and revelation. When I hear something that seems really unwise, I test it again and again before I launch out. The flesh will try to use your "freedom" to get you to do things you shouldn't do. And now that the Enemy knows you are trying to walk with God and tune in to your heart, he'll play the ventriloquist and try to deceive you there. Any "word" or suggestion that brings discouragement, condemnation, accusation— that is not from God. Neither is confusion, nor any counsel that would lead you to disobey what you do know. Reject it all, and carry on in your journey. Yes, of course, God needs to convict us of sin, warn us of wrong movements in the soul, discipline us for our own good—but the voice of God is never condemning (Rom. 8:1), never harsh or accusing. His conviction brings a desire for repentance; Satan's accusation kills our hearts (2 Cor. 7:10). (p. 106)

4. Get alongside those who walk with God.

With whom have you walked? With whom might you want to?

Hopefully you will find a few folks who walk with God who will also walk with you through the seasons of your life. But honesty—and Scripture—forces me to admit they are a rare breed. Few there are who find them. All the more reason for you to enlarge the number by becoming someone who walks with God and teaches others how.

> Look to those who have walked with God down through the ages. Certainly that is why the Bible is given to us. If God had intended it to be a textbook of doctrine, well, then, he would have written it like one . . . But . . . it's overwhelmingly a book of stories—tales of men and women who walked with God. Approach the Scriptures not so much as a manual of Christian principles but as the testimony of God's friends on what it means to walk with him through a thousand different episodes. When you are at war, when you are in love, when you have sinned, when you have been given a great gift—this is how you walk with God. Do you see what a different mind-set this is? It's really quite exciting. (pp. 107–8)

TO CLARIFY

The Christian's interest in Scripture has always been in hearing God speak, not in analyzing moral memos. The common practice is to nurture a listening disposition—the involving ear rather than the distancing eye—hoping to become passionate hearers of the Word rather than cool readers of the page.

Listening and reading are not the same thing. The intent in reading Scripture, among people of faith, is to extend the range of our listening to the God who reveals himself in word, to become acquainted with the ways in which he has spoken in various times and places, along with the ways in which people respond when he speaks. (Eugene Peterson, *Working the Angles*)

And there are those who have walked with God since the canon of Scripture closed. Here is an Athanasius, a Bonaventure, a Julian of Norwich, a Brother Lawrence, an A. W. Tozer—here is how they walked with God. When it comes to time and place, temperament and situation, they could not be more different. Julian lived in a cloister; Tozer lived in Chicago. Athanasius fled to the desert; Lawrence worked in the kitchen. But there is a flavor, a tang, an authenticity to their writings that underlies whatever it is they are trying at the moment to say. Here is someone who knew God, really knew him. This is what it's like to walk with God, and that is what it's like as well. (p. 108)

And so, where is your heart as you end this chapter? Can you put into a sentence or two what God has said to you through this chapter?

What was the most stirring idea in this chapter for you?

What questions or desires do you want to take to God?

How do you see yourself walking with God? What will you be doing differently?

CHAPTER SEVEN

RECEIVING HIS INTIMATE COUNSEL

They dress the wound of my people
as though it were not serious.

—GOD (JER. 6:14)

HEART MONITOR

How's your heart today? Pausing for a few moments, consider whether there is anything you would like to do for your heart prior to digging in (taking a stroll, enjoying beauty, music, stillness in his presence, a conversation).

Where's the Battle raging in your life? Do you need to deal with anything that would reduce this time to simply "getting through" another chapter?

And who are you again? Though the newness of the concept may embarrass you, what's your mythic role/place in the unfolding story of God?

A First Reaction

A Mythic Parable

And being very tired and having nothing inside him, he felt so sorry for himself that the tears rolled down his cheeks. What put a stop to all this was a sudden fright. Shasta discovered that someone or somebody was walking beside him. It was pitch dark and he could see nothing. And the Thing (or Person) was going so quietly that he could hardly hear any footfalls. What he could hear was breathing. His invisible companion seemed to breathe on a very large scale . . .

If the horse had been any good—or if he had known how to get any good out of the horse—he would have risked everything on a breakaway and a wild gallop. But he knew he couldn't make that horse gallop. So he went on at a walking pace and the unseen companion walked and breathed beside him. At last he could bear it no longer. "Who are you?" he said, scarcely above a whisper.

"One who has waited long for you to speak," said the Thing. Its voice was not loud, but very large and deep . . .

"Oh please—please do go away. What harm have I ever done you? Oh, I am the unluckiest person in the whole world!" Once more he felt the warm breath of the Thing on his hand and face. "There," it said, "that is not the breath of a ghost. Tell me your sorrows." Shasta was a little reassured by the breath: so he told how he had never known his real father or mother and had been brought up sternly by the fisherman. And then he told the story of his escape and how they were chased by lions and forced to swim for their lives; and of all their dangers in Tashbaan and about his night among the tombs and how the beasts howled at him out of the desert. And he told about the heat and thirst of their desert journey and how they were almost at their goal when another lion chased them and wounded Aravis. And also, how very long it was since he had had anything to eat.

"I do not call you unfortunate," said the Large Voice. "Don't you think it was bad luck to meet so many lions?" said Shasta. "There was only one lion," said the Voice. "What on earth do you mean? I've just told you there were at least two the first night, and . . ." "There was only one; but he was swift of foot." "How do you know?"

"I was the lion."

And as Shasta gaped with open mouth and said nothing, the Voice continued. "I was the lion who forced you to join with Aravis. I was the cat who comforted you among the houses of the dead. I was the lion who drove the jackals from you while you slept. I was the lion who gave the Horses the new strength of fear for the last mile so that you should reach King Lune in time. And I was the lion you do not remember who pushed the boat in which you lay, a child near death, so that it came to shore where a man sat, wakeful at midnight, to receive you."

"Then it was you who wounded Aravis?"

"It was I."

"But what for?"

"Child," said the Voice, "I am telling you your story, not hers."

(C. S. Lewis, *The Horse and His Boy*) (pp. 110–12)

What does the story stir in you? Does it open up some aspect of the Christian life to you . . . or some aspect of your life?

❧ THE BIG IDEAS

FIRST, your life is a story, and over the course of that story your core convictions have formed down deep in your heart. Much of what resides down there is not true—that's just what happens when we grow up in a fallen world.

SECOND, getting the truth down into our hearts—and dislodging the other beliefs that have settled there—is the work of the Counselor, the Spirit of God who now walks with us. That's why Jesus sent him to us.

THIRD, we must ask God to show us our hearts *are* good, and that our hearts *do* matter to him.

Big Idea 1: WHAT YOU BELIEVE ABOUT YOUR HEART WAS HANDED TO YOU BY OTHERS

Our life is a story. A rather long and complicated story that has unfolded over time. There are many scenes, large and small, and many "firsts." Your first step; your first word; your first day of school. There was your first best friend; your first recital; your first date; your first love; your first kiss; your first heartbreak. If you stop and think of it, your heart has lived through quite a story thus far. And over the course of that story your heart has learned many things. Some of what you learned is true; much of it is not. Not when it comes to the core questions about your heart and the heart of God. Is your heart good? Does your heart really matter? What has life taught you about that? Imagine for a moment that God is walking softly beside you. You sense his presence, feel his warm breath. He says, "Tell me your sorrows." What would you say in reply? (p. 112)

Is your heart good? Does your heart really matter? What *has* life taught you about that?

I know this is a hard question to just jump into. Most of us don't even really know what we believe about our hearts, let alone where that came from. I know I have believed my heart was bad, partly because I'm still so shocked by the teaching of the new covenant that tells me it is good. My surprise at that truth reveals to me what I have believed. But there is more. It was only last month that some new clarity came to me. Over the years I've been nagged with this sense that "it's not enough." Whenever I give a talk, I sense that "it wasn't good enough; it wasn't long enough." The same thing happens when I write a book—even this book. It's not clear enough; it's not well written. Even in a simple conversation with a friend, I'll often walk away feeling that it wasn't good enough.

As I thought about my life, I began to see how there have been these key moments when the people I loved just up and left for no reason at all. My dad, through his alcoholism, and Debbie, my first love (the story I told in this chapter). It happened with friends too. They left, or sent me away, with no explanation. What settled in my heart was "There must be something wrong with me. I must not be enough to make them stay." Years upon years later, I am still nagged by this sense that whatever I am offering, it's not enough.

It might help to pray and ask Jesus to reveal to you: "What do I believe about my heart, Lord? Do I think it's bad? Do I think it really matters?" (John)

Imagine for a moment that God is walking softly beside you. You sense his presence, feel his warm breath. He says, "Tell me your sorrows." What would you say in reply? Just let your heart go there. God is beside you. He wants to know. "Tell me your sorrows." What *would* you say?

Remember, the purpose of this thing called the Christian life is that our hearts might be restored and set free. That's the deal. That's what Jesus came to do, by his own announcement. Jesus wants Life for us, Life with a capital *L*, and that Life comes to us through our hearts. But restoring and releasing the heart is no easy project. God doesn't just throw a switch and poof—it's done. He sends his Counselor to walk with us instead. That tells us it's going to be a *process*. All sorts of damage has been done to the heart over the years, all sorts of terrible things taken in—by sin, by those who should have known better, and by our Enemy who seeks to steal and kill and destroy the image bearers of God. At best, "hope deferred makes the heart sick" (Prov. 13:12). Certainly, there's been a bit of that in your life. "Even in laughter the heart may ache" (Prov. 14:13), which is to say, things may look fine on the outside, but inside it's another story. (p. 113)

Can you relate to that? When you're at work, or at church, or at a social gathering, does your "outside" match your "inside"? Do you sometimes put on a good front that says, "Everything is fine"—and is that how you feel *inside*?

We're told to "trust in the LORD" with all our hearts (Prov. 3:5), but frankly, we find it hard to do. Does trust come easily for you? I would *love* to trust God wholeheartedly. Why is it almost second nature to worry about things? (p. 113)

Does trust come easily for you? Are you at peace, full of a deep confidence in God? Or do you find yourself fretting about things as you drive along in your car, or when you wake in the middle of the night? What is your heart worried about these days?

You see, we don't really develop our core convictions so much as they develop within us, when we are young. Down deep, in the inmost parts they form, down in deep water, like the shifting of the continental plates. Certainly, we'd reject the more disabling beliefs if we could; but they form when we are vulnerable, without our really knowing it, like a handprint in wet cement, and over time the cement hardens and there you have it. Think of it this way: Have you always known down deep inside, down to the tip of your toes, that *your* heart is good and that *your* heart matters to God? (p. 114)

Well—have you? What have you believed about your heart over the years? Who taught you that?

To Clarify

I believe that our hearts endure two kinds of damage over the years. One is open assault; the other is more subtle "misunderstanding." The Scriptures give us examples of both, and life does too. If that doesn't seem clear to you, it might help to begin by acknowledging that God's command was that everyone in your life would have loved you truly (see Mark 12:31). You were meant to grow up in a world where everyone knew you and loved you. But you did not. This is a fallen world, full of fallen people. Furthermore, it is a world at war. You were not loved as you were meant to be. The question is, how did that shape your convictions about yourself?

Joseph had a dream, and when he told it to his brothers, they hated him all the more. He said to them, "Listen to this dream I had: We were binding sheaves of grain out in the field when suddenly my sheaf rose and stood upright, while your sheaves gathered around mine and bowed down to it." His brothers said to him, "Do you intend to reign over us? Will you actually rule us?" And they hated him all the more because of his dream and what he had said. (Gen. 37:5–8)

. . . Joseph stands out, as we were all meant to stand out, each in his or her own way. Instead of celebrating his glory, his brothers want to destroy it. A common story, I'm sorry to say. The worst blows typically come from family. That's where we start our journey of the heart, and that's where we are most vulnerable. (pp. 114–115)

Does it still come as a surprise to you that you were *meant* to stand out, to shine? What did your family celebrate about you? What did they affirm, encourage, applaud?

I feel bad answering this, because I don't want to sound as though I am always down on my family. I think they tried to love me. But to be honest, I'm having a hard time remembering what they celebrated about me—and that is telling. They liked the fact that I was smart and got good grades. They liked my performances in the theater. But I don't think they really knew me. They all seemed too busy, caught up in their own battles, taken out by their own assaults. To this day, I don't think they even know me, let alone celebrate what they do not know or understand. (John)

So Joseph went after his brothers and found them near Dothan. But they saw him in the distance, and before he reached them, they plotted to kill him. "Here comes that dreamer!" they said to each other. "Come now, let's kill him and throw him into one of these cisterns and say that a ferocious animal devoured him. Then we'll see what comes of his dreams." (Gen. 37:17–20)

. . . What we learned from our parents and siblings about our heart defines us the rest of our days; it becomes the script we live out, for good or for ill. Cinderella's father calls her "a little stunted kitchen wench which my late wife left behind," and her stepmother sees her as "much too dirty; she cannot show herself!" What do you suppose she learned about her heart from growing up in *that* home?

. . . There is David, whose heart of glory rises like the sun, full of faith and courage when he sees that no one will take on Goliath. Though he is only a youth, untrained for war, he is outraged that an "uncircumcised Philistine" has dared to taunt the armies of the living God. He announces, "Let no one lose heart on account of this Philistine; your servant will go and fight him" (1 Sam. 17:32). David's oldest brother was among the soldiers of Israel who *should* have had the heart to face Goliath but rehearsed his excuses instead. His cowardice is exposed by David's bravery after he lashes out: "Why have you come down here? And with whom did you leave those few sheep in the desert? I know how conceited you are and how wicked your heart is; you came down only to watch the battle" (1 Sam. 17:28). Ah, family. (pp. 114–16)

Joseph is actually physically assaulted because he has a glory that outshines his brothers'. Cinderella is shamed by words. So is David. His brother openly (and unfairly) accuses him of having a wicked heart. Are you aware of how your heart has been assaulted over the years? Can you recall words and events when you were shamed, belittled, accused, assaulted?

Even Jesus endured this sort of assault—not the open accusation that he had a wicked heart, but the more subtle kind, the seemingly "innocent" arrows that come through "misunderstanding" . . . I think we can relate to that. Did your family believe in you? Some did—but far too many more believe in the person *they* wanted you to be. Did they even notice your heart at all? Have they been thrilled in your choices, or has their disappointment made it clear that you just aren't what you're supposed to be? (p. 117)

How would you answer that? *Did* your family believe in you? *Did* they even notice your heart at all? Have they been thrilled in your choices, or has their disappointment made it clear that you just aren't what you're supposed to be?

My parents and sisters do not believe in Christ, and that makes this very, very hard, because Jesus is the center of everything I hold dear. Misunderstanding is the constant theme of my relationships with my family, simply because they don't get it. That makes things hard to explain—why we won't come for Christmas, why we raise our boys the way we do. We can't even begin to explain the Battle we are in, and how demanding our calling can be. Bottom line, my family doesn't even begin to understand my heart. So no, there is no affirmation of who and what I am, or what I'm doing. Just pleasant remarks and conversation about the weather. (John)

I'm not big on computer games personally. But my eldest son, Sam, is an absolute crackerjack at them. It's a point of tension in our relationship. I don't think he ought to spend so much time there, and he thinks he's not given enough. Though I try to hide my distaste because I know how much he loves playing Off Road Fury and Delta Force, it's pretty obvious when I never play with him. Just yesterday Sam said to me, "You and Mom don't like computer games, so I feel like you don't like me." Ouch. I missed a part of his glory, shamed a part of his heart. How many an artist has been crushed in a family that prefers a "rational" approach to life? How many an engineer dismissed by a family of musicians? How many of us are lost in life simply because no one in our early world saw our glory and affirmed it? (p. 118)

Think about the course your life has taken. Was it your desire—or your family's desire for you? Do you even know what to do with your life?

Do you know the glory of your heart? If so, how did you come to that knowledge? If not (and that's most of us), what does that tell you about how well your family saw and affirmed and helped to nourish your heart's glory?

Misunderstanding is damaging, more insidious because we don't identify it as an attack on our hearts. How subtly it comes, sowing doubt and discouragement where should have been validation and support. There must be something wrong with us.

This idea—that most of us believe there must be something wrong with us—might come as a surprise. So let me ask you this: Imagine that a gathering has been called of all the people in your life—family relations, friends, church acquaintances, coworkers. They have something they want to say to you. Once everyone is seated in the room, the host stands up and says, "Now, we all know why we're here. It's time to be honest—only honesty will help [you]. So I want each of you to rise and tell us what you have seen beneath the masks that [you] wears. Go ahead—be completely candid and forthright." Does the idea of this gathering sound inviting and happy to you? If not, what do you fear they will say?

To Clarify

"How long, O men, will you turn my glory into shame?" (Ps. 4:2). These blows aren't random or incidental. They strike directly at some part of the heart, turn the very thing God created to be a source of celebration into a source of shame. And so you can at least begin to discover your glory by looking more closely at what you were shamed for. Look at what's been assaulted, used, abused. As Bernard of Clairvaux declared, "Through the heart's wound, I see its secret." (p. 118)

This is an amazing truth, one which I wish I had spent more time on in the book: that through the very wounds of your life, you can find the secret to your glory. Or put another way, through the very things you have felt shame for (or embarrassment, or just thought they weren't much at all), you can see your glory.

A young man came to Craig for some counseling because he didn't know what to do with his life. He had earned two Ph.D.'s but hadn't a clue what to do now that school was over. He didn't seem to have any passions, desires, dreams. Then he remembered that once—long ago—he loved music. He loved playing the piano. One day his father came in from the gym (the boy was not an athlete like his dad) and called him a "faggot" for playing music. He stopped playing the piano that day, and has been lost ever since. His glory—music—turned to shame.

What dreams and desires, what gifts or unique qualities have you been wounded over, felt shame or embarrassment about, or just thought weren't worth much? It might help to ask Jesus: "Show me, Lord, where my glory has been wounded, where I have lost heart over the years."

Big Idea 2: DISLODGING FALSE BELIEFS IS THE WORK OF THE COUNSELOR

For years now I've lived with the fear that at some point, everyone is going to leave, and I will be left alone. For no reason I can say, in no way I can prevent, I am going to wind up alone. I can't really explain why, but I know it's my fault. It lingers there, down under the surface, like a chronic backache or a low-grade fever. But it colors everything I say and do; it shapes every relationship. I remain guarded, distant. I feel I ought to do more, be more. So it becomes a self-fulfilling prophecy. And I'm sick of it.

I parked the car and simply let the tears come, allowed the memories to take me to the place in my heart that was pierced by the loss of those I loved, "loved but did not understand in my youth," as Norman MacLean said. Somehow, being in the old neighborhoods again, smelling all the old familiar smells, hearing the voices of the past, brought this unhealed place to the surface. And Jesus walked softly beside. (pp. 119–20)

What issues have pinned down your heart over the years? What places do you need to go back to, if not literally (as I did, driving to the old neighborhood), then certainly emotionally? What places in the heart do you need to invite Jesus into? Maybe it's a memory, or a certain time in your life. Or maybe it's something nagging you now, an unnamed fear, an anxiousness, anger, or discouragement you can't seem to shake. Can you name them here?

And right now, ask Jesus to come and meet you in these places. One by one, ask him to speak to you here, to bring the truth down into your inmost being.

This is what he did for Karen:

> On Monday, I ventured over to the park for just some time in beauty. The sun was slowly making its way down, and as I watched, my heart just ached to receive what God was whispering: "Karen, yes your heart is good, ever since you let me come in and dwell there . . . but." And I stopped there. It was getting dark, and I had things to do. So I made my way back to my car . . . slowly. A few steps later, I heard God say that He wouldn't let me leave without hearing the rest of it. But I kept walking, until I just couldn't go any further—dang it. I knew that He wanted to be with me in a place that was not comfortable, was not "safe," not in my car where no one could see me. Oh no . . . it had to be there in a public wilderness. For that was part of the freedom that my heart needed—release from trying to "save" face and release from caring so much what people think of me (the lies that killed my heart as a leader in the church).
>
> The tears of grief flowed freely down my face. He began to show me and I let Him. I was reminded of all of the recurring assaults and with each arrow He spoke to me His shield, "You see, Karen, that lie? That was the assault to keep you from connecting. That lie? That one was to make you fearful and anxious. That brutal arrow? That was to keep you from glorifying ME. Ah . . . but Karen, in the places where those lies targeted . . . your heart was good. It is good." As God spoke, I wept. I've so needed to grieve where my heart has been lost. I've needed to find it! I got mad at the lies and strategies that Satan has used on me. Wow. Little did I know that a huge part of the freedom God has been aching for me to experience would come from asking our Abba to "show me that my heart is good." (p. 123)

Go with God into these places. What do you hear him say?

Big Idea 3: WE MUST ASK GOD TO SHOW US OUR HEARTS ARE GOOD

Notice also that Jesus asks Peter the penetrating question three times—once for every betrayal. Peter is hurt by it, and that is the point. The lessons that have been laid down in pain can be accessed only in pain. Christ must open the wound, not just bandage it over. Sometimes he'll take us there by having an event repeat itself years later, only with new characters in the current situation. We find ourselves overlooked for a job, just as we were overlooked by our parents. Or we experience fear again, just as we felt those lonely nights in our room upstairs. These are all *invitations* to go with him into the deep waters of the heart, uncover the lies buried down there, and bring in the truth that will set us free. Don't just bury it quickly; ask God what he is wanting to speak to.

There are two things we need to know, maybe above all else. We need to know that our heart is good, and that our heart matters to God. I've found that for most folks, this is what's been most assaulted; this is what we most doubt. We can't just talk ourselves into this; Jesus must show us. He must take us there, as he did with Peter. So ask him. Ask God to show you that your heart is good, and that you do matter to him. (p. 122)

This may be the single most life-changing thing you get out of the whole book. You must ask him. Ask God to show you that your heart is good, and that you do matter to him. And don't just sort of throw it up there, a quick question you fear he won't answer. Ask like the persistent widow—*stay with the question* until God reveals to you what you so desperately need to hear. It might begin to come right now. It might take a week or two. When God speaks, *write it down.* Then ask him again the next week. Ask God to reveal to you that the new covenant is true. Your heart is good. And your heart matters. Deeply.

I want to be careful, lest I have painted a wrong picture here. This stream of Counseling doesn't just flow to us directly from Christ, *only* from him. It flows through his people as well. We need others—and need them deeply. Yes, the Spirit was sent to be our Counselor. Yes, Jesus speaks to us personally. But often he works through another human being. The fact is, we are usually too close to our lives to see what's going on. Because it's *our* story we're trying to understand, we sometimes don't know what's true or false, what's real and imagined. We can't see the forest for the trees. It often takes the eyes of someone to whom we can tell our story, bare our souls. The more dire our straits, the more difficult it can be to hear directly from God. (pp. 124–125)

Have you begun to cultivate a relationship or two where you can bare your heart to others, and they to you? If so, where do you need to go next in your relationship? What do you need to bring before them in your own heart's journey? Is there something from this guidebook you need to share with them, ask their thoughts about? And if you do not have a relationship like that, why not? What are you waiting for? Ask God who that person might be. For some, you might want to seek out a trained counselor to spend some time with.

It was more than a little unnerving. I'd been seen; I'd been found out. But not as a disappointment, not as a bad heart exposed. Rather, it was my glory that had been seen, and it was being asked for. What do you do with *that*?

Over the course of several months my whole system of perfectionism-so-as-not-to-be-seen unraveled. *Maybe* . . . the thought began to creep in . . . *maybe the world has been wrong about me.* "The world has been wrong about you. They've hated your glory—just as the Evil One hates the glory of God. But we need your gift. Come forth." (pp. 125–26)

Let that thought sink in for a moment: *maybe the world has been wrong about me* (meaning, you, dear reader). What goes on in your heart?

And so, where is your heart as you end this chapter? Can you put into a sentence or two what God has said to you through this chapter?

What was the most stirring idea in this chapter for you?

What questions or desires do you want to take to God?

To bring this time to a close, pray.

CHAPTER EIGHT

DEEP RESTORATION

He heals the brokenhearted
and binds up their wounds.
—PSALM 147:3

HEART MONITOR

How's your heart today? Pausing for a few moments, consider whether there is anything you would like to do for your heart prior to digging in (taking a stroll, enjoying beauty, music, stillness in his presence, a conversation).

Where's the Battle raging in your life? Do you need to deal with anything that would reduce this time to simply "getting through" another chapter?

And who are you again? Though the newness of the concept may embarrass you, what's your mythic role/place in the unfolding story of God?

A First Reaction

A Mythic Parable

> For at that moment a curious little procession was approaching—eleven Mice, six of whom carried between them something on a litter made of branches, but the litter was no bigger than a large atlas. No one has ever seen mice more woebegone than these. They were plastered with mud—some with blood too—and their ears were down and their whiskers drooped and their tails dragged in the grass, and their leader piped on his slender pipe a melancholy tune. On the litter lay what seemed little better than a damp heap of fur; all that was left of Reepicheep. He was still breathing, but more dead than alive, gashed with innumerable wounds, one paw crushed, and, where his tail had been, a bandaged stump.
>
> "Now, Lucy," said Aslan.
>
> Lucy had her diamond bottle out in a moment. Though only a drop was needed on each of Reepicheep's wounds, the wounds were so many that there was a long and anxious silence before she had finished and the Master Mouse sprang from the litter. His hand went at once to his sword hilt, with the other he twirled his whiskers. He bowed.
>
> "Hail, Aslan!" (C. S. Lewis, *Prince Caspian*) (pp. 128–29)

What does the story stir in you? Does it open up some aspect of the Christian life to you . . . or some aspect of your life?

To Clarify

I (John here) recognize that this chapter might be the newest, or strangest, set of ideas yet. To accept that we are the brokenhearted, that there are young and unhealed places in us may seem weird at first, or strange. Some of my closest friends and companions in ministry felt that way up until the last few weeks—until Christ came and revealed broken places in them, and healed them. Now they have no doubts! So my editor urged me to find a biblical example of Christ coming and healing a broken part, a young place inside of someone. "It will help a lot of your readers if you can find a scriptural example of this kind of work in a person's life." Of course, there are no such stories we can directly point to.

But before you dismiss it on those grounds, consider this: there are no stories in the New Testament of a church service passing an offering plate, either. Yet we have accepted that as common practice in our churches. We do have the *principle* of "Each man should give what he has decided in his heart to give" (2 Cor. 9:7), but we do not find the Sunday offering plate being passed in the Bible.

Another example would be the daily "quiet time" many Christians have come to accept as standard fare for the Christian life. You won't find that in the Bible, either. What you will find are principles of hiding the Word in your heart (Ps. 119:11) and Christ rising in the morning to pray (Mark 1:35). But nowhere in the Bible are we told to have a "quiet time" every day.

Maybe a more important example would be modern medicine. Cancer is not addressed in the Bible by name, nor are we told by God how to cure it. That is something we have discovered, by his grace, through our experimentation with the world God has given us. We have found cancer in people (many people, I'm sorry to say). And we are learning how to treat it. Certainly we're not going to dismiss cancer research and treatment because we don't find a direct example in the Bible.

In other words, the Bible is *authoritative* but not *exhaustive*. On every subject the Bible does address, it is reliable and wholly true. It is authoritative. But the Bible does not address every subject, such as cancer research. It is not *exhaustive*. There are many arenas of human life in which we look to the Bible for principles, and then learn through experience how to take care of things. The stream of deep restoration is one of those arenas. We have the truth given to us that we are the brokenhearted. We have the promise that Christ will come to heal our brokenness. Let us now journey with him into that healing.

❀ THE BIG IDEAS

FIRST, we are a house divided. We are not wholehearted. According to Christ, we are the brokenhearted.

SECOND, Jesus offers more than forgiveness to us. He offers to heal our brokenness.

THIRD, we must go there with Christ, allow him in, let him do his healing work. It is something he offers to do for us, but we must accept it, walk with him there.

Big Idea 1: WE ARE THE BROKENHEARTED

> The Spirit of the Sovereign LORD is on me,
>   because the LORD has anointed me
>   to preach good news to the poor.
> He has sent me to bind up the brokenhearted,
>   to proclaim freedom for the captives
>   and release from darkness for the prisoners.
>   (Isa. 61:1)

Isaiah 61:1 is the Scripture that Jesus himself points to on the very first day he launches his public ministry (Luke 4:14–21). Of all the passages from the Old Testament prophesies about the Messiah that Jesus might have referred to, this is the passage he chose. This is what Jesus wants us to understand as his primary mission. What do you think he means by the "brokenhearted" and the "captive"?

In our culture, we tend to use the word *brokenhearted* to refer to someone who has lost something dear to him or her. Speaking of a parent who is grieving the loss of his child in an automobile accident, we might say, "He's absolutely brokenhearted about it." Or we might be thinking of a lover who has been told that the one she loves no longer loves her: "She's got a broken heart right now." It's a figure of speech we use, a kind of picture or poetic expression to try to describe deep sorrow or desolation. But that is not what Jesus is talking about.

> When Isaiah promised that the Messiah will come to heal the brokenhearted, he was not speaking poetically. The Bible does use metaphor, as in when Jesus says, "I am the gate" (John 10:9). Of course, he is not an *actual* gate like the kind you slammed yesterday; he has no hinges on his body, no knob you turn. He is using metaphor. But when Isaiah talks about the brokenhearted, God is not using metaphor. The Hebrew is *leb shabar* (*leb* for "heart," *shabar* for "broken").
>
> Isaiah uses the word *shabar* to describe a bush whose "twigs are dry, they are broken off" (27:11); to describe the idols of Babylon lying "shattered on the ground" (21:9), as a statue shatters into a thousand pieces when you knock it off the table; or to describe a broken bone (38:13). God is speaking literally here. He says, "Your heart is now in many pieces. I want to heal it."
>
> The heart can be broken—literally. Just like a branch or a statue or a bone. Can you name any precious thing that *can't*? Certainly, we've seen that the mind can be broken—or what are all those mental institutions for? Most of the wandering, muttering "homeless" people pushing a shopping cart along have a broken mind. The will can be broken too. Have you seen photos of concentration camp prisoners? Their eyes are cast down; something in them is defeated. They will do whatever they are told. But somehow we have overlooked the fact that this treasure called the heart can also be broken, *has* been broken, and now lies in pieces down under the surface. (pp. 131–32)

Is that a new thought to you—that your heart can actually be broken?

To Clarify

Your heart was made for the paradise of Eden. That is the world, the environment for which your soul was made. A world of peace and love and security, a world of beauty and intimacy without one awful moment throughout your entire life.

But that is not the world your heart entered when you were born. Far, far from it.

Picture a precious child, a little girl or boy about three or four years old, wandering through the midst of a war: Vietnam, perhaps, or Omaha Beach, or Gettysburg. Certainly, he or she would be frightened. After witnessing firsthand bodies being blown apart, arms and legs everywhere, the screams of the dying, it's probably safe to say he or she would be emotionally scarred. And I think it is also safe to say that the child will not pass through that battlefield without getting hit as well.

It is an awful image, but not far from the reality of what the human heart undergoes when it finds itself not in Eden at all, but in this world at war, this awful spiritual battle. You just don't get through this life without being wounded, and most likely, suffering brokenness. This is not the habitat for which your heart was made.

It doesn't take a major assault like sexual abuse to create a broken heart, by the way. This is so important to understand, for many good people assume they haven't any real brokenness because they haven't endured the horrors they read about in the paper or watch on TV. Depending on the age or circumstances, it can be an embarrassing moment like stuttering in front of the class or hearing a harsh word from your mother. The bottom line is, Jesus speaks as though we are all the brokenhearted. We would do well to trust his perspective on this. (p. 134)

Jesus speaks as though we are *all* the brokenhearted. My reasoning is simple: Christ didn't come only for those of us who have recently lost a loved one. He came for us all. In his own words, he came to seek and save the lost (Luke 19:10). He came for you and for me, and he calls us the brokenhearted and the captive. What does Jesus assume about us, then?

THE SIGNS OF BROKENNESS

I expect that all of us at one time or another have said, "Well, part of me wants to, and another part of me doesn't." You know the feeling—part of you pulled one direction, part of you the other. Part of me loves writing and genuinely looks forward to a day at my desk. But not all of me. Sometimes I'm also afraid of it. Part of me fears that I will fail—that I am simply stating what is painfully obvious, or saying something vital but incoherent. I'm drawn to it, and I also feel ambivalent about it. Come to think of it, I feel that way about a lot of things. Part of me wants to go ahead and dive into friendship, take the risk. I'm tired of living alone. Another part says, *Stay away—you'll get hurt. Nobody really cares anyway.* Part of me says, *Wow! Maybe God really is going to come through for me.* Another voice rises up and says, *You are on your own.* (p. 129)

Don't you feel sometimes like a house divided? How do you experience that?

Take your little phobias. Why are you afraid of heights or intimacy or public speaking? All the discipline in the world wouldn't get you to go skydiving, share something really personal in a small group, or take the pulpit next Sunday. Why do you hate it when people touch you or criticize you? And what about those little "idiosyncrasies" you can't give up to save your life? Why do you bite your nails? Why do you work so many hours? Why do you get irritated at these questions? You won't go out unless your makeup is perfect—why is that? Other women don't mind being seen in their grubbies. Something in you "freezes" when your dad calls—what's that all about? You clean and organize; you demand perfection—did you ever wonder *why*? (pp. 129–130)

Are you aware of your little (and maybe not so little) quirks and fears and phobias? Where *do* those phobias and habits you can't break come from? How do you explain that?

She told me that when she was a very young girl of four or five, she had a little toy puppy that was her playmate. You know how that goes—they went everywhere together. The two of them had tea parties. He went to kindergarten in her backpack. He took all the family trips with her. This little puppy—Scruffy was his name—had the place of honor in her bedroom, upon her pillow every night. He was her special friend. That is, until the day her father in a fit of rage ripped the head off Scruffy while she stood crying before him, begging her daddy not to hurt him. It was the kind of blow that shatters a little girl's heart. It's not just about a stuffed animal, of course. The assault brought terror into her relationship with her daddy, cast a shadow over her whole young world, shattered all security. Fifty-some years later she is unable to make herself stop collecting puppies, and she cannot tell you why. (p. 131)

Are there things you find yourself doing—or things you find you cannot do—and you aren't really able to explain why? Surely there are things you do that you cannot provide a reasonable explanation for. Those of you unable to resist a jelly donut—certainly, that is a hunger for more than sweets. Love, perhaps? Comfort? The drive that keeps you late at the office—what is it that you are hoping for? Approval? For someone to finally say, "We're so very proud of you"?

What about emotions that come out of nowhere? For years, I had this anger problem that would surface out of the blue. I also mentioned in the book my struggle with fear—I felt fear a lot over the years, but for no apparent reason. For others, it might be sadness, or shame, or the feeling that any moment now they are going to be exposed. And you?

Yet another indication of a house divided is the "on again, off again" personality. One day you are kind; the next day you are sullen and angry. One day you are inspired by Christ, captured for his purposes; the next day, you are completely driven by the world. Sure—we all have bad days. Lord knows, PMS and traffic jams can bring on some dramatic changes. But I'm talking about a pattern that is repeated again and again. (pp. 133–34)

Are you aware of a shift in who you are and how you are, one day "on," the next day "off"? How does that look for you—can you describe it?

Big Idea 2: CHRIST OFFERS US MORE THAN FORGIVENESS; HE OFFERS TO HEAL US

For this people's heart has become calloused;
    they hardly hear with their ears,
    and they have closed their eyes.
Otherwise they might see with their eyes,
    hear with their ears,
    understand with their hearts
and turn, *and I would heal them.* (Matt. 13:15, emphasis added) (p. 134)

"And I would heal them." What do you suppose Jesus means by this?

> That's a different offer from: "And I would forgive them." It's a different offer from: "And I will give them a place in heaven." No, Jesus is offering *healing* to us. Look at what he does to people who are broken. How does he handle them? The blind are able to see like a hawk. The deaf are able to hear a pin drop. The lame do hurdles. The corroding skin of the leper is cleansed and made new. The woman with the issue of blood stops hemorrhaging. The paralyzed servant hops out of bed. They are, every last one of them, healed. (pp. 134–35)

Does it help you to see in all those cases what Jesus wants to do for you? What is the common theme—what does each of them receive?

> *This is just so beautiful—how come I've never paid much attention to this before? I think I was taught that the miracles of Christ were just these things he did to prove he was God. But no—there is a theme here. Such a beautiful theme. Jesus restores each of them, right where they need restoring. He comes for his creation and renews it. Wow. (John)*

Now follow this closely: everything Jesus *did* was to illustrate what he was trying to *say*. Here—look at this—this is what I'm offering to do for you. Not just for your body, but more important, for your soul. I can heal your heart. I can restore your soul.

> The LORD is my shepherd, I shall not be in want.
>> He makes me lie down in green pastures,
> he leads me beside quiet waters,
>> he restores my soul. (Ps. 23:1–3)

He heals the brokenhearted
and binds up their wounds. (Ps. 147:3)

Heal me, O LORD, and I will be healed;
save me and I will be saved,
for you are the one I praise. (Jer. 17:14)

For you who revere my name, the sun of righteousness will rise with healing in its wings. (Mal. 4:2)

He welcomed them and spoke to them about the kingdom of God, and healed those who needed healing. (Luke 9:11)

For some reason, this has been lost in much of the recent offerings of the church. Perhaps it has been our pride, which has kept us from admitting that we are broken. Lord knows, I've done that for years—probably am still doing it now. Perhaps it is our fear of getting our hopes up; it seems too good to be true. Perhaps it's been the almost total focus on sin and the Cross. But the Scripture is abundant and clear: Christ came not only to pardon us, but also to heal us. He wants the glory restored. So, put the book down for just a moment, and let this sink in: Jesus can, and wants to, heal your heart. What does that rouse in you? Is it hope? Is it cynicism? Is it "I tried that—it doesn't work"? (pp. 135–36)

Big Idea 3: WE MUST GO THERE WITH CHRIST, ALLOW HIM IN, LET HIM DO HIS HEALING WORK

Reread the story I told of the healing I received from Christ in the mountains (pp. 137–139). What does it stir in you?

We simply invoke His Presence, then invite Him into our hearts. He shows us our hearts. In prayer for the healing of memories, we simply ask our Lord to come present to that place where we were so wounded (or perhaps wounded another). Forgiving others, and receiving forgiveness, occurs. In prayer for the healing of the heart from fears, bitterness, etc., we see primal fears as well as lesser ones dealt with immediately: those fears that the sufferer often has not been aware of, never been able to name—they only know that their lives have been seriously restricted and shaped because of them. (Leanne Payne, *The Healing Presence*) (p. 140)

TO CLARIFY

In the book I tried to lay out the simple, beautiful process Jesus has taught our ministry team for the healing of broken hearts. I don't want you just to have an inspiring thought or a good theory. I want your heart to be healed!

It may be that Christ wants to take you there, right now, to heal some things in your heart. We've found that sometimes it can be done alone, just you with Christ. We've also found that sometimes it helps to have the presence of another person, or several people, to pray and listen alongside you as you listen to Christ.

Walk with God through this, and he will show you what is best for you.

Step 1: Get Away with God

> The LORD is my shepherd, I shall not be in want.
> He makes me lie down in green pastures,
> he leads me beside quiet waters,
> he restores my soul. (Ps. 23:1–3)

Take some time, at least an hour, to get away to a safe and quiet place. Your bedroom, perhaps. Somewhere you won't be disturbed (unplug the phone!).

When we are in the presence of God, removed from distractions, we are able to hear him more clearly, and a secure environment has been established for the young and broken places in our hearts to surface. We ask God to surround us with his presence. We give ourselves back over to him, come under his authority, for as Paul warns, it is possible to lose connection with our Head, who is Christ (Col. 2:19). We declare the authority of Jesus over our hearts, for he made our hearts (Ps. 33:15) and he has redeemed our hearts (Rom. 2:29).

Jesus, I come into your presence now, and I ask you to surround me. I come under your authority and your claim upon my life. I give myself to you—body, soul, and spirit. I give my heart to you, in every way—including the broken places in me. I declare your authority over my heart, for you made my heart and you have redeemed my heart. (p. 141)

Step 2: Give Christ Access to Your Brokenness

"If you hear me calling and open the door, I will come in." (Rev. 3:20 NLT)

We invite Christ in. We ask Jesus to come into the emotion, the memory, this broken place within us. We give him permission; we give him access. We open the door to this particular place in our hearts . . . Truth be told, there are probably many broken places within us. Stay with one at a time, the one connected with the event or the emotion or the habit you can't seem to escape. Ask Jesus to bring his light there. "For God, who said, 'Let light shine out of darkness,' made his light shine in our hearts" (2 Cor. 4:6). *What's going on here, Jesus? What is this all about? Shine your light in my heart.* Ask him to make it clear to you.

Jesus, I invite you into this broken place within me (this wound, this memory). I give you total access to my heart. Come, Lord, shine your light here. Reveal to me all that is going on here. What is this about, Jesus? Come and show me, meet me here, in this place. (pp. 141–142)

TO CLARIFY

Sometimes [Jesus] will take us back to a memory, a time and place where a shattering blow was given. Other times he will make us aware of a young place in our hearts. You might feel an emotion you haven't felt for years. Let it come. You might remember something you had long forgotten. Let it come. You might even "hear," inside your heart, a young place speaking—a sentence like *I'm lonely*, or *Why did they do that to me?* Let it come.

Just the other evening, Stasi and I were in the living room together, reading.

She told me she had been sad for several days, but she wasn't sure why. There wasn't anything sad going on in her life—quite the contrary. It had been a good several weeks with many blessings. But as she prayed about it, tuned in to her heart, she became aware of a place in her heart that felt as if it was weeping . . . We asked Jesus about it, and sure enough, there was a part of Stasi's heart, about seventeen years old, that was grieving. We asked Jesus to come in and lead us in prayer for this brokenness. (p. 142)

Step 3: Ask Jesus What He Is Saying to This Wounded Part of You

We ask Jesus what he is saying to this wounded part of us, listening, as Payne puts it, "for the healing word that God is always sending to the wounded." He will often bring words of love and kindness, or comfort, specifically to this place in our hearts: "You have the words of real life" (John 6:68 *The Message*). Sometimes he will ask a question: *Why are you frightened?* or *Will you let me heal you?* He is drawing this place in our hearts out from the shadows, out from hiding; he is bringing our brokenness into the place of assurance.

Jesus, come and lead me in healing this brokenness in my heart. Speak to me here, Lord. What are you saying to me? Give me ears to hear and eyes to see what you are revealing. Let no other voice speak but you, my Lord Jesus, and you alone. (pp. 142–143)

TO CLARIFY

Listening to your own heart, and to the voice of Jesus within you, takes a little time. If you don't hear anything at first, don't be discouraged. Pray again, and wait. He might bring up another memory; or you might simply feel another strong emotion. Go back to Step 2, and invite Christ in. Then ask him to speak, and listen.

I find so often that the key to hearing Christ is simply this: trusting that I *do* hear. He wants to speak, and you are his child. Trust that you do hear.

When we are doing this together, what Christ will often do is "speak" through the one who is acting as facilitator. I will hear what Jesus is wanting to say to the broken place in another, and I will speak out loud what I am hearing in my heart. The other person is freed to listen to what his brokenness is saying in reply.

Step 4: Confess

Now, I think it is safe to say that we all have mishandled these places in our hearts. We push them down, as I did. Or we turn to something or someone we hope will bring comfort, like food or sex. If we have done that, Jesus will often make that clear to us as we pray. As he does, we confess our sins, renounce them (often a great act of the will), and ask him to cleanse our hearts (1 John 1:9).

Jesus, forgive me for the ways I've mishandled my brokenness. You alone make me dwell in safety. Forgive me for all my self-protection and self-redemption, and for all my false comforters. (You'll want to renounce specific sins you are aware of here.) *Cleanse my heart of every sin by your shed blood.* (p. 143)

TO CLARIFY

Step 4 is not an "essential" one. I include it only because sometimes, Jesus will ask us to forgive the person who injured us, to forgive ourselves, or even . . . to forgive him. Not that he has sinned, but sometimes there is a resentment down inside that he let it happen, didn't protect us. So I include this step only because sometimes it's needed.

This is true for Step 5 as well. Jesus may "jump" straight to Step 6. Simply go with him. He is the Shepherd.

Step 5: Break Any Agreement You've Made with the Lies of the Enemy

Oftentimes these young and broken places have become sites of spiritual strongholds. (This will make a great deal more sense after you read the next chapter.) All of the streams flow together for our healing; we must use the stream of Warfare as well. Our sins give the Enemy a certain claim to our lives (Rom. 6:16). As we renounce any sin, we also renounce any claim we've given to Satan in our lives. This often comes in the form of "agreements"—Satan has suggested something to us, and we have said, "Yes." He might have said, Don't ever trust anyone, or Your heart is bad— never show it to anyone, or You are dirty . . . lustful . . . addicted and never will get free. Whatever we have agreed with, we renounce those agreements. We ask God to cleanse us by the blood of Christ; we command our Enemy to flee (James 4:7).

I now break every agreement I have made with Satan and his lies. (Get specific here. What have you believed, bought into?) *I renounce any claim I have given to my Enemy, and in the name of Jesus I command him to flee.* (pp. 143–144)

To Clarify

Like Step 4, this is not an essential step. Sometimes Jesus just goes straight to healing.

But just the other day, Craig and I were praying for a young place in his heart, a place that was crying out for healing. As we prayed and listened to Jesus, Craig couldn't hear anything inside. I asked in prayer, "What is keeping this young place from talking to Jesus? Why are you afraid to come out?" What Craig sensed in that moment, the *impression* he felt inside, was *Because there are bullies here.* He shared that with me, and I knew that the "bullies" were foul spirits present, trying to prevent healing. Out loud (this will make more sense after the next two chapters) I brought the cross of Christ against them, sent them to Christ for their judgment. As soon as I did, Craig was able to access the young and wounded place within him.

Again, this doesn't happen all the time—not even most of the time—but it does come up, and that is why I offer this guidance in Step 5.

Step 6: Ask Christ to Heal This Place in Your Heart

And then we ask Jesus to do for us the very thing he said he came to do: we ask him to heal this brokenness, to bind up our hearts. Sometimes he will ask us to take his hand in this shattered place, follow him into his heart and his presence within us.

These places are often isolated from the life and the love of God in us; he draws them back into his presence and heals them through union with himself, *in* our hearts. Our part is to listen and follow where he is leading, and to welcome that part of our heart home. This is so important because many of us *sent* that part away. We welcome back the despised, forsaken part, just as Jesus embraces us.

Jesus, come now and do as you promised to do—heal my broken heart and set me free. (Listen here for what Jesus is saying. He will guide.) *Bring this place into your love and healing, bring this place home. I welcome your healing, and I welcome this part of my heart home. Come, bind me up and make me whole.* (p. 144)

GOING ON WITH GOD

"Healing prayer," says Payne, "is not the 'instant fix,' nor the bypassing of slow and steady growth. It is that which clears the path and makes such progress possible." Brokenness keeps so many people from walking the path that God has for them. Make straight paths for your feet, so that the limb which is lame may not be put out of joint, but rather be healed (Heb. 12:13 NASB). As long as we have these unhealed places within us, these rifts in the soul, we will find it next to impossible to live in freedom and victory. No matter how much we demand of ourselves, applying discipline and doctrine, it will not work. It has not worked. Those places keep undermining us at crucial moments, cutting us off at the knees . . . We desperately need the stream of Healing, so that we may go on to walk this journey with Christ. (pp. 144–145)

And so, where is your heart as you end this chapter? Can you put into a sentence or two what God has said to you through this chapter?

What was the most stirring idea in this chapter for you?

What questions or desires do you want to take to God?

To bring this time to a close, pray.

CHAPTER NINE

SPIRITUAL WARFARE:
FIGHTING FOR YOUR HEART

Awake, awake, O Zion,
  clothe yourself with strength . . .
Shake off your dust;
  rise up, sit enthroned, O Jerusalem.
Free yourself from the chains on your neck,
  O captive Daughter of Zion.

—GOD (ISA. 52:1–2)

HEART MONITOR

Take an inventory before you begin. How's your heart doing? Where are you right now? What are you feeling . . . thinking . . . wanting?

What's been nagging at you today? Any accusation . . . discouragement . . . distraction? Are you even aware of what's been nipping at your heels?

So, how has the war against your heart manifested itself in your life recently? Are you beginning to see the assaults more clearly now?

What thoughts have you begun to entertain about your crucial role in God's plan? Who are you, really?

Finally, a simple prayer:

Jesus, I ask you now for the Spirit of wisdom and revelation. By your Spirit, guide me through my work here, so that I may know you, really know you, and the life you offer me. Open the eyes of my heart, Lord. I want all that you have for me here. I want, and ask for, my whole heart back.

A FIRST REACTION

A MYTHIC PARABLE

Wolfgang Amadeus Mozart was a glorious man. An image bearer. You remember from your youth the little song "Twinkle, Twinkle, Little Star"? Mozart wrote that melody when he was three. He composed his first symphony when he was twelve.

And Mozart's music has *endured,* enchanting the world for centuries. He is probably played more often than any other classical composer. Yet this brilliant man died young—we don't really know how or why. Impoverished, alone, his body was dumped in a common grave. The movie *Amadeus* is Peter Shaffer's attempt to tell that tale.

It's a story of genius and jealousy, leading to murder. Shaffer creates a villain worthy of the devil himself in the character of the court composer Salieri. A musician of lesser note, Salieri is tormented by envy of Mozart's greatness. Like Joseph's brothers. He embodies what must have been Lucifer's jealousy of God's glory, which brought the angel to his ruin. There is a remarkable scene in the film that depicts the day Mozart's wife brings his music to Salieri, in hopes of getting her husband a job. She does not yet know that he is a wolf in sheep's clothing. Glancing through the pages of Mozart's portfolio, Salieri is captivated by the work of his rival's hand.

> Salieri: These . . . are *originals?*
> Frau Mozart: Yes, sir. He doesn't make copies.
> *[As the astonished composer begins to read the sheets before him, he narrates the tale.]*
> Salieri: Astounding. It was actually . . . beyond belief. These were first, and *only,* drafts of music. But they showed no correction of any kind. Not one. He had simply written down music already finished . . . in his *head!* Page after page of it, as if he were just taking dictation! And music . . . finished like no music is ever finished. Displace one note and there would be diminishment. Displace one phrase and the structure would fall. It was clear to me . . . that sound I had heard in the Archbishop's palace had been no accident. Here again was the very voice of God. I was staring through the cage of those meticulous ink strokes at an absolute beauty.
> *[Salieri is enraptured, and the sheets fall to the floor from his limp hands.]*
> Frau Mozart: Is it not good?
> Salieri: *[Clearly wounded]* It is . . . miraculous.
> Frau Mozart: Yes . . . he's very proud of his work. So you will help us?
> *[Sullen, determined, Salieri simply leaves the room in silence. The scene shifts to his private chambers. Salieri is taking down a crucifix from the wall and placing it in the fire.]*
> Salieri: From now on we are enemies, You and I. Because You choose for

Your instrument a boastful, lustful, smutty, infantile boy . . . and give me only the ability to recognize the Incarnation. Because You are *unjust . . . unfair . . . unkind!* I will block You. I swear it. I will hinder and harm Your creature here on earth as far as I am able. *[Shaking his fist in the air]* I will ruin Your incarnation. (pp. 147–49)

What does the story stir in you? Does it open up some aspect of the Christian life to you . . . or some aspect of your life?

❀ THE BIG IDEAS

FIRST, you have an Enemy. The story of your life is the story of the long and brutal assault on your heart by the one who knows what you could be and fears it.

SECOND, as the Father of Lies (John 8:44), Satan is trying to get you to agree with him. We must beware of making agreements, and we must break the ones we have made.

THIRD, there is no escaping this war. Just because you refuse to believe it doesn't make it go away.

Big Idea 1: YOU HAVE AN ENEMY

Think of it—why does every story have a villain?

Little Red Riding Hood is attacked by a wolf. Dorothy must face and bring down the Wicked Witch of the West. Qui-Gon Jinn and Obi-Wan Kenobi go hand to hand against Darth Maul. To release the captives of the Matrix, Neo battles the powerful "agents." Frodo is hunted by the Black Riders. (The Morgul blade that the Black Riders pierced Frodo with in the battle on Weathertop—it was aimed at his heart.) Beowulf kills the monster Grendel, and then he has to battle Grendel's mother. Saint George slays the dragon. The children who stumbled into Narnia are called upon by Aslan to battle the White Witch and her armies so that Narnia might be free. (pp. 150–51)

Why, do you suppose, does every story have a villain?

Every story has a villain because *yours* does. You were born into a world at war. When Satan lost the battle against Michael and his angels, "he was hurled to the earth, and his angels with him" (Rev. 12:9). That means that right now, on this earth, there are hundreds of thousands, if not millions, of fallen angels, foul spirits, bent on our destruction. And what is Satan's mood? "He is filled with fury, because he knows that his time is short" (v. 12). So what does he spend every day and every night of his sleepless, untiring existence doing? "Then the dragon was enraged at the woman and went off to make war against . . . those who obey God's commands and hold to the testimony of Jesus" (v. 17). He has you in his crosshairs, and he isn't smiling. (p. 151)

Do you live like that? What have you seen as the Enemy's work in your life this week? Last week? This year? Do you look at life as a battle for your heart at all?

> I will go before you
>   and will level the mountains;
> I will break down gates of bronze
>   and cut through bars of iron.
> I will give you the treasures of darkness,
>   riches stored in secret places,
> so that you may know I am the LORD,
>   the God of Israel, who summons you by name. (Isa. 45:2–3)

Doesn't the language of the Bible sometimes sound . . . overblown? Really now—God is going to level mountains for us? We'd be happy if he just helped us get through the week. What's all that about breaking down gates of bronze and cutting through bars of iron? I mean, it sounds heroic, but, well, who's really in need of that? This isn't ancient Samaria. We'd settle for a parking place at the mall. Now, I like the part about treasures of darkness and riches stored in secret places—it reminds me of *Treasure Island* and Long John Silver and all that. What boy hasn't wanted to find buried treasure? And, in fact, those associations make the passage seem like fantasy as well—good poetry, meant to inspire. But not much more. (pp. 149–50)

Well—doesn't it? Doesn't the language of the Bible sometimes sound overblown? What have you done with all those passages like the one from Isaiah 45?

What if we looked at the passage through the eyes of the heart? That language makes perfect sense if we are living a reality on the mythic level of *Amadeus* or *The Lord of the Rings*. In those stories, gates must be broken down, riches are hidden in darkness, and precious friends must be set free. If we *are* in an epic battle, then the language of the Bible fits perfectly. Things are not what they seem. We are at war. That war is against your heart, your glory. (p. 150)

How *would* it change your understanding of life—your life—if you did see it "mythically," that is to say, spiritually? If you saw yourself caught up in something on the order of *The Lord of the Rings*?

Once more, look at Isaiah 61:1:

> He has sent me to bind up the brokenhearted,
> to proclaim freedom for the captives
> and release from darkness for the prisoners.

This is God's personal mission for his people; the offer is for us all. So, we must all be held prisoner to some form of darkness. We didn't know it—that's proof enough. In the darkness we can't see. And what is this hidden treasure? Our *hearts*—they are the treasures hidden by darkness. They are not darkness; they are *hidden* by darkness, pinned down, held away in secret places like a hostage held for ransom. Prisoners of war. That is a given. That is assumed. The question is not, *Are* we spiritually oppressed, but *Where* and *How*? (p. 150)

Where, and how, are you being attacked? Where does your heart feel pinned down? Where is life just not coming to you?

Big Idea 2: SATAN, THE FATHER OF LIES, IS TRYING TO GET YOU TO AGREE WITH HIM

Satan is called in Scripture the Father of Lies (John 8:44). His very first attack against the human race was to lie to Eve and Adam about God, and where life is to be found, and what the consequences of certain actions would and would not be. He is a master at this. He suggests to us—as he suggested to Adam and Eve—some sort of idea or inclination or impression, and what he is seeking is a sort of "agreement" on the part of human beings. He's hoping we'll buy into whatever he's saying, offering, insinuating. Our first parents bought into it, and look what disaster came of it. But that story is not over. The Evil One is still lying to us, seeking our agreement every single day.

Your heart is good. Your heart matters to God. These are the two hardest things to hang on to. I'm serious—try it. Try to hold this up for even a day. *My heart is good. My heart matters to God.* You will be amazed at how much accusation you live under. (pp. 152–53)

Has it been easy to hold on to those two truths—that your heart is good and does matter to God? Do you believe it right now? And if not (as for most of us), if that does not put a spring in your step, what do you hear or feel about your heart these days?

And where do you suppose that has come from?

You have an argument with your daughter on the way to school; as you drive off, you have a nagging sense of, *Well, you really blew that one.* If your heart agrees—*Yeah, I really did*—without taking the issue to Jesus, then the Enemy will try to go for more. *You're always blowing it with her.* Another agreement is made. *It's true. I'm such a lousy parent.* Keep this up and your whole day is tanked in about five minutes. The Enemy will take any small victory he can get. It moves from *You did a bad thing* to *You are bad.* Or weak. Or ugly. Or prideful. You know how it goes. After a while it just becomes a cloud we live under, accept as normal.

My friend Aaron decided to get into shape. He went out and took a run. First, the Enemy tried discouragement to get him to quit. *Look how far you have to go. You can't do this—you'll die out there. Give it up.* Aaron thought, *Gee—it is a long way. I'm not sure I can do this.* But then he recognized what was going on and pressed into it. The attack became more personal, more vicious. He was running along, and he was hearing stuff like this: *You're just a fat pig. You always have been.* A gorgeous woman in fabulous shape approached from the other direction. *She'd never be attracted to a slob like you.* "By the time I got back to my car," he said, "it felt like I'd been assaulted. But this time, I knew what it was and I won." (p. 153)

Have you had something like this happen to you recently? An argument, and afterward you felt so lousy? Or some accusation coming against you?

This sort of thing goes on all the time. But unlike Aaron, most of the time we don't recognize it as attack. At first it tends to be vague—not voices in the head, not an obvious assault, but more of a "sense" we have, an impression, a feeling that comes over us. The power of *suggestion*. (p. 153)

What has that been for you?

Now that I stop and think about it, I begin to see something. Two things: First, there's been this sense lately of "You're an arrogant man. You're prideful." I even got an e-mail accusing me of that two days ago, now that I think about it. Hmm. There's a theme going on here. Jesus—what do you think?

And then, second, there's been this really persistent "sense" that I'm going to blow it with this ministry, I'm headed for some fall. Some secret sin is just waiting to take me down—at least, that's the accusation. In my moments of clarity, I know it's not true. But more than not, I think I've been agreeing with it. I've been letting this cloud camp over me. It's really stolen my joy, that's for sure. (John)

If you are having trouble taking in all of this, let me ask you: Have you had this experience? Something bad happens, and you start telling yourself what a jerk you are. Do you really think the source of that is just you? Or God? Think about it this way: Who would take the most delight in it? Take it all real slow if you need to. Start by simply entertaining the notion that the source might be something besides your "low self-esteem." (p. 155)

The whole plan is based on agreements. When we make those agreements with the demonic forces suggesting things to us, we come under their influence. It becomes a kind of permission we give the Enemy, sort of like a contract. The bronze gates start clanging shut around us. I'm serious—maybe half the stuff people are trying to "work through" in counseling offices, or pray about in their quiet times, is simply agreements they've made with the Enemy. Some foul spirit whispers, *I'm such a stupid idiot,* and they agree with it; then they spend months and years trying to sort through feelings of insignificance. They'd end their agony in about a week if they'd treat it for the warfare it is, break the agreement they've made, send the Enemy packing. (pp. 154–55)

What "agreements" have you been making with the Enemy? Do you want to stop making those now?

Jesus, forgive me for agreeing with the Father of Lies. I confess that I've been going right along with Satan's accusations. (Be specific: In what way? What agreements?) Here and now I draw the line. I break every agreement that I have made with Satan and his workers. I renounce those lies. (Again, be specific). I make my total agreement with you, Jesus. Strengthen me to walk in the light, in your truth. (John)

Big Idea 3: THERE IS NO ESCAPING THIS WAR

Your enemy the devil prowls around like a roaring lion looking for someone to devour. Resist him, standing firm in the faith, because you know that your brothers throughout the world are undergoing the same sort of sufferings. (1 Peter 5:8–9)

What is God, speaking here through the apostle Peter, assuming about your life?

And the picture of a lion, seeking to devour: how fierce is that image? What does it intend to describe?

Reread the story about Stephen on pages 157–59. What does it stir in you?

If you deny the battle raging against your heart, well, then, the thief just gets to steal and kill and destroy. Some friends of mine started a Christian school together a few years ago. It had been their shared dream for nearly all their adult lives. After years of praying and talking and dreaming, it finally happened. Then the assault came . . . but they would not see it as such. It was "hassles" and "misunderstanding" at first. As it grew worse, it became a rift between them. A mutual friend warned them of the warfare, urged them to fight it as such. "No," they insisted, "this is about *us*. We just don't see eye-to-eye." I'm sorry to say their school shut its doors a few months ago, and the two aren't speaking to each other. Because they refused to fight it for the warfare it was, they got taken out. I could tell you many, many stories like that. (p. 159)

Think of an event where you saw someone lose some part of his life that meant a great deal to him: a marriage, perhaps, or a job or ministry. Did he see the work of the enemy in it? Did you?

Listen carefully: any movement toward freedom and life, any movement toward God or others, *will be opposed*. Marriage, friendship, beauty, rest—the thief wants it all. (p. 154)

What "life" have you been hoping for, but it never seems to come through? Something at home or at work? Trying to lose weight, or make a friend? Have you considered that the thief might be involved?

> This is what the LORD says,
>
>   he who appoints the sun to shine by day,
>
> who decrees the moon and stars to shine by night,
>
> who stirs up the sea so that its waves roar—
>
> the LORD Almighty is his name. (Jer. 31:35)

I was reading the prophet Jeremiah a few weeks ago when I ran across a passage that referred to God as "the LORD Almighty." To be honest, it didn't resonate. There's something too religious about the phrase; it sounds churchy, sanctimonious. The *Lawd Almiiiighty*. It sounds like something your grandmother would say when you came into her kitchen covered in mud. I found myself curious about what the *actual* phrase means in Hebrew. Might we have lost something in the translation? So I turned to the front of the version I was using for an explanation. Here is what the editors said:

> Because for most readers today the phrases "the Lord of hosts" and "God of hosts" have little meaning, this version renders them "the Lord Almighty" and "God Almighty." These renderings convey the sense of the Hebrew, namely, "he who is sovereign over all the 'hosts' (powers) in heaven and on earth, especially over the 'hosts' (armies) of Israel." (p. 160)

Write down what these two phrases evoke in you, what they tell you about God:

The Lord Almighty

The God of angel armies

> The Hebrew means "the God of angel armies," "the God of the armies who fight for his people." *The God who is at war.* Does "Lord Almighty" convey "the God who is at war"? Not to me, it doesn't. Not to anyone I've asked. It sounds like "the God who is way up there but still in charge." Powerful, in control. The God of angel armies sounds like the one who would roll up his sleeves, take up sword and shield to break down gates of bronze, and cut through bars of iron to rescue me. Compare "Joe is a good man who is in control" to "Joe is a Navy Seal." It changes the way you think about Joe and what he's up to. (pp. 160–61)

Compare these two ways of thinking about God. He is good. He is a warrior, like a Navy Seal. What's the difference? Which God have you lived with all these years?

Why don't "most readers today" understand about the God of angel armies? Could it be because we have abandoned a warfare worldview?

For that matter, who has kept the new covenant so effectively under wraps that most Christians still believe their hearts are evil? It happened again just the other night—a leader in their church told friends of mine, in a very direct way, "The heart is desperately wicked." Dear God—they hold to that lie as a core doctrine of their *faith*. To say your heart is good still sounds like heresy. (p. 161)

Doesn't it? I mean, before you read *Waking the Dead,* had you been taught in your church that the heart is central, and that the heart is good?

How would you be received by most of your Christian friends if you told them your heart was good, and you were following it?

Why do most Christians still believe their hearts are bad? Why do so few know that this is a world at war?

Where are the Four Streams? The Religious Spirit has turned discipleship into a soul-killing exercise of principles. Most folks don't even know they can walk with God, hear his voice. He's stigmatized counseling as a profession for sick patients, and so the wounds of our hearts never get healed. He's taken healing away from us almost entirely so that we sit in pews as broken people feeling guilty we can't live the life we're supposed to live. And he takes warfare and mocks it, stigmatizes it as well so that most of the church knows almost nothing about how to break strongholds, set captives free.

Finally, the Religious Spirit makes it next to impossible for a person to break free by spreading the lie that *there is no war*. Be honest. How many Christians do you know who practice spiritual warfare as a normal, necessary, daily part of the Christian life? Some of my dearest friends pull back from this stream and sort of cast a concerned look over me when I suggest it's going on. Onward, Christian soldiers, marching as to war? You've got to be kidding me. We gave up the hymn not so much for reasons of musical fashion but because we felt ridiculous singing it, as you do when asked to sing "Happy Birthday" in a restaurant to a perfect stranger. We don't sing it 'cause it ain't true. We have acquiesced. We have surrendered without a fight. (p. 162)

Do you begin to see how Satan has taken Christianity and turned it into a subtle counterfeit? What other ways do you see this happening?

So here's a bottom-line test to expose the Religious Spirit: if it doesn't bring freedom and it doesn't bring life, it's not Christianity. If it doesn't restore the image of God and rejoice in the heart, it's not Christianity. (p. 163)

Go ahead—hold this test up to the various Christian groups and programs you've been a part of. List the programs here, and ask: Does it bring freedom and does it bring life? Does it restore the image of God and rejoice in the heart?

That evening after sunset the people brought to Jesus all the sick and demon-possessed. The whole town gathered at the door, and Jesus healed many who had various diseases. He also drove out many demons. (Mark 1:32–34)

God anointed Jesus of Nazareth with the Holy Spirit and power, and . . . he went around doing good and healing all who were under the power of the devil, because God was with him. (Acts 10:38)

For this purpose the Son of God was manifested, that He might destroy the works of the devil. (1 John 3:8 NKJV)

What do these passage tell you about the ministry of Jesus?

And so, if we are to carry on his ministry, what do they tell you about what our lives should involve?

TO CLARIFY

Read the first ten chapters of the gospel of Luke, asking yourself this question:

How often does Jesus confront foul spirits to set his people free? How aggressive is he in the Battle?

The reason I bring this up is that if you want the real deal, if you want the life and freedom that Jesus offers, then you are going to have to break free of this religious fog in particular. "It is for freedom that Christ has set us free. Stand firm, then, and do not let yourselves be burdened again by a yoke of slavery" (Gal. 5:1). (p. 163)

Are you beginning to see more clearly the battle for your heart and your life? Are you willing to fight for it?

And so, where is your heart as you end this chapter? Can you put into a sentence or two what God has said to you through this chapter?

What do you need to do for your heart and your freedom?

CHAPTER TEN

SETTING HEARTS FREE:
INTEGRATING THE FOUR STREAMS

Can plunder be taken from warriors,
*   or captives rescued from the fierce?*
But this is what the LORD says:
"Yes, captives will be taken from warriors,
*   and plunder retrieved from the fierce;*
I will contend with those who contend with you,
*   and your children I will save.*
I will make your oppressors eat their own flesh;
*   they will be drunk on their own blood, as with wine.*
Then all mankind will know
*   that I, the LORD, am your Savior,*
*   your Redeemer, the Mighty One of Jacob.*
                                    —ISAIAH (49:24–26)

HEART MONITOR

Take an inventory before you begin. How's your heart doing? Where are you right now?
What are you feeling . . . thinking . . . wanting?

What's been nagging at you today? Any accusation . . . discouragement . . . distraction? Are you even aware of what's been nipping at your heels?

So, how has the war against your heart manifested itself in your life recently? Are you beginning to see the assaults more clearly now?

What thoughts have you begun to entertain about your crucial role in God's plan? Who are you, really?

Finally, a simple prayer:

Jesus, I ask you now for the Spirit of wisdom and revelation. By your Spirit, guide me through my work here, so that I may know you, really know you, and the life you offer me. Open the eyes of my heart, Lord. I want all that you have for me here. I want, and ask for, my whole heart back.

A FIRST REACTION

A MYTHIC PARABLE

They were about twice our height, and armed to the teeth. Through the visors of their helmets their monstrous eyes shone with a horrible ferocity. I was in the middle position, and middle giant approached me. My eyes were busy with his armor, and I was not a moment in settling the mode of attack. I saw that his body-armor was somewhat clumsily made, and that the overlappings in the lower part had more play than necessary, and I hoped that, in a fortunate moment, some joint would open a little, in a visible and accessible part. I stood till he came near enough to aim a blow at me with the mace, which has been, in all ages, the favorite weapon of giants, when, of course, I leaped aside, and let the blow fall upon the spot where I had been standing. Full of fury, he made at me again; but I kept him busy, constantly eluding his blows, and hoping thus to fatigue him. He did not seem to fear any assault from me, and I attempted none as yet. At length, as if somewhat fatigued, he paused for a moment, and drew himself slightly up; I bounded forward, foot and hand, ran my rapier through to the armor of his back, let go the hilt, and passing under his right arm, turned as he fell, and flew at him with my saber. At one happy blow I divided the band of his helmet, which fell off, and allowed me, with a second cut across the eyes, to blind him. After which I clove his head.

I stood exhausted amidst the dead, after the first worthy deed of my life.

I searched the giants, and found the keys of their castle, to which I repaired . . . I released the prisoners, knights and ladies, all in a sad condition, from the cruelties of the giants. (*Phantastes,* George MacDonald) (pp. 164–65)

What does it stir in you—awaken you to?

❋ THE BIG IDEAS

FIRST, we were created to Rule. With fierce mastery.

SECOND, spiritual warfare is one of the primary arenas in which God teaches us how to Rule.

THIRD, it takes all Four Streams to set a heart free, find the life Christ offers.

Big Idea 1: WE WERE CREATED TO RULE—WITH FIERCE MASTERY

> Let's come back for a moment to original glory, the glory of God given to us when we were created in his image. So much light could be shed on our lives if we would explore what we were *meant* to be before things started going wrong. What were we created to *do*? What was our original job description? (p. 165)

Over the years, what have you thought about that—about what mankind was created to do? How would you have answered someone who asked, "Why did God make us?"

> Then God said, "Let us make man in our image, in our likeness, and let them rule over the fish of the sea and the birds of the air, over the livestock, over all the earth, and over all the creatures that move along the ground." So God created man in his own image, in the image of God he created him; male and female he created them. God blessed them and said to them, "Be fruitful and increase in number; fill the earth and subdue it. Rule." (Gen.1:26–28)

> And let them *rule*. Like a foreman runs a ranch or like a skipper runs his ship. Better still, like a king rules a kingdom, God appoints us as the governors of his domain. We were created to be the kings and queens of the earth (small *k*, small *q*). Hebrew scholar Robert Alter has looked long and hard at this passage, mining it for its riches. He says the idea of *rule* means "a fierce exercise of mastery." It is active, engaged, passionate. It is *fierce*. I suppose such language doesn't really fit if we were created to spend our days singing in the choir ("I may never march in the infantry"). But it makes perfect sense if we were born into a world at war. God says, "It will not be easy going. This is no Sunday school hour. Rule fiercely in my name." We were meant to rule, as he—the God of angel armies—rules. (pp. 165–66)

Does this put things in a new light for you? What's your reaction to the idea that you were created to rule, with a fierce mastery, just as the God of angel armies rules?

I have been way too passive. Way too passive. My approach to this whole Christian life thing has pretty much been "God is in charge. If he wants it done, he'll get it done." I did not—until recently—see my role as being all that important. I mean, live a moral life, yes. Rule over part of his kingdom? Never even crossed my mind. (John)

Now—what will be our role in the kingdom of God to come? What does he have in store for us in the future? Let's take the parable of the talents as one example. A landowner is going away for a while, and he appoints his servants to take care of the place while he's gone. Some do, and some don't. When he returns, he rewards those who ruled well in his absence by giving them even greater authority over his estate. He says, "Well done, good and faithful servant! You have been faithful with a few things; I will put you in charge of many things" (Matt. 25:21). Jesus teaches that in the coming kingdom, we will be promoted to positions of authority, and we will reign with him there. The ranch hand is promoted to foreman; the manager gets the vice president's office; the prince becomes king.

To drive the point home, Jesus follows this parable with another, a story about some sheep and goats. The sheep are the good guys in this tale, and their reward is really amazing. Jesus says, "Then the King will say to those on his right, 'Come, you who are blessed by my Father; take your inheritance, the kingdom prepared for you since the creation of the world'" (Matt. 25:34). He doesn't say, "Good job. Now, come and sing songs in heaven forever." He gives them an entire kingdom to rule over—a kingdom waiting for them since the beginning of time. That was the plan all along. That's why we read in Revelation 22:5, "And they [meaning the saints] will reign for ever and ever." We will rule, just as we were always meant to. (pp. 166–67)

Is that how you've understood your future—that you will *not* stand in a never-ending church service, singing songs, but you will be given a part of God's kingdom to rule over? What does that promise evoke in you?

To Clarify

To gain a deeper understanding of our eternal kind of life in God's present kingdom, we must be sure to understand what a *kingdom* is. Every last one of us has a "kingdom"—or a "queendom," a realm that is uniquely our own, where our choice determines what happens. Here is a truth that reaches into the deepest part of what it means to be a person . . . we are made to "have dominion" . . . This is the core of the likeness or image of God in us and is the basis of the destiny for which we were formed. We are, all of us, never-ceasing spiritual beings with a unique and eternal calling to count for good in God's great universe.

Our "kingdom" is simply *the range of our effective will.* Whatever we genuinely have the say over is in our kingdom. And our having the say over something is precisely what places it within our kingdom. In creating human beings God made them to rule, to reign, to have dominion in a limited sphere. Only so can they be persons.

(Dallas Willard, *The Divine Conspiracy*)

Big Idea 2: SPIRITUAL WARFARE IS A PRIMARY ARENA IN WHICH GOD TEACHES US HOW TO RULE

And in the meantime? What is God up to with us in the meantime? Training us to do what we're made to do: rule. In the gospel of Luke, chapter 10, there is a sort of test flight for this whole idea. Christ appoints seventy-two of his disciples—not the apostles, just regular folks like you and me—to go out and prepare the way for his ministry. (The story will make more sense if we remember that his ministry is healing the brokenhearted and setting the captives free.) Jesus sets the stage by saying, "I am sending you out like lambs among wolves" (10:3). In other words, this could get vicious. It's no rummage sale.

Now, when the seventy-two return, they are blown away by what happened: "The seventy-two returned with joy and said, 'Lord, even the demons submit to us in your name'" (10:17). Christ gives his followers his authority, and they go out to set captives free. Jesus listens carefully to the report, and then he says, "I saw Satan fall like lightning from heaven" (v. 18). In other words, "You see, you guys? It works! It *works*! Satan's days are numbered!" But the battle is not over; it's just beginning to heat up. Jesus then goes on to say, "I have given you authority to . . . overcome all the power of the enemy" (v. 19). There's more to be done. This was only a trial run. After his resurrection, Jesus sends us *all* out to do what he did: "As the Father has sent me, so I send you" (John 20:21 NRSV). And he gives us his authority to do it: "All authority in heaven and on earth has been given to me. Therefore go" (Matt. 28:18–19). Why else would he have given us his authority if we weren't supposed to *use* it? (pp. 167–68)

In the meantime. Meaning, our days here on earth. What *did* you think we were supposed to be up to "in the meantime"?

The attitude of so many Christians today is anything *but* fierce. We're passive, acquiescent. We're acting as if the battle is over, as if the wolf and the lamb are now fast friends. Good grief—we're beating swords into plowshares as the armies of the Evil One descend upon us. We've bought the lie of the Religious Spirit, which says, "You don't need to fight the Enemy. Let Jesus do that." It's nonsense. It's unbiblical. It's like a private in Vietnam saying, "My commander will do all the fighting for me;

I don't even need to fire my weapon." We are *commanded* to "resist the devil, and he will flee from you" (James 4:7). We are told, "Your enemy the devil prowls around like a roaring lion looking for someone to devour. Resist him" (1 Peter 5:8–9); "Fight the good fight" (1 Tim. 1:18); "Rescue those being led away to death" (Prov. 24:11).

Seriously, just this morning a man said to me, "We don't need to fight the Enemy. Jesus has won." (p. 168)

Have you heard or sensed that passive attitude among the Christians in your circles? Where have you seen it—maybe even in your life?

Yes, Jesus has won the victory over Satan and his kingdom. *However,* the battle is not over. Look at 1 Corinthians 15:24–25: "Then the end will come, when he [Jesus] hands over the kingdom to God the Father after he has destroyed all dominion, authority and power. For he must reign until he has put all his enemies under his feet." *After* he has destroyed the rest of the Enemy's works. *Until* then, he must reign by bringing his enemies under his feet. Jesus is still at war, and he calls us to join him. (p. 168)

Think about the different aspects of your "realm": your home, your work, your place in the world. Are you "ruling" them well, meaning, are you fighting to see that God's will is done in each, as it is done in heaven?

Read again this story from the life of Catherine of Sienna that helped Leann Payne see the battle for her heart and trained her to fight it. In the story Catherine has gone up to a secret place to pray:

As she began to pray, her ears were assaulted by blasphemous words, and she cried out to God, "Oh, look, Lord, I came up here to give you my day. Now look what is happening." And the Lord said, "Does this please you, Catherine?" "Oh no, Lord," she said. And the Lord said, "It is because I indwell you that this displeases you so." These words brought instant understanding of my plight . . . I also knew that the problem was not a state or condition of my mind or my heart, but that it was harassment from without, from the accuser of my soul. I knew beyond all shadow of a doubt that "Greater is he who is in you, than he who is in the world." I then cried out to God, "Take it away, Lord. Send this filthy, horrible thing away." But the Lord said, "No, you do it." It was then that I learned spiritual authority. Centered in God and He in me, I took authority over the evil spirit when it manifested itself and commanded it to leave. After several months of this, a concentrated training in moving from the center where Christ dwells, I was utterly free of this harassment. (pp. 168–69)

What are you struck by?

Notice, first, that the victory came when she realized that those awful thoughts were *not* from her; her heart is good. The assault came from *outside,* from the Enemy. That is the turning point, when we begin to operate as if the heart is good, and we are at war. Second, notice that Jesus told *her* to send it away. "You do it." *We* must exercise our authority in Christ. *We* are to resist. Finally, notice that it took several months of battle for a final victory. During that period of time, she was not blowing it, nor was God holding out on her. It was *training.* We are made to rule. We need to learn how. Spiritual warfare is a great deal of our training. (p. 169)

Can you recognize now some recent event or situation in your life that you thought was just a hassle or maybe a trial, which in fact is exactly what Payne describes above: attack by the Enemy that God is permitting in order for you to learn how to rise up, take charge, fight back? Maybe it would help to ask Jesus to reveal it to you.

Big Idea 3: IT TAKES ALL FOUR STREAMS TO SET A HEART FREE, FIND THE LIFE CHRIST OFFERS

It might be good to come back to John 10:10 one more time:

> The thief comes only to steal and kill and destroy;
> I have come that they may have life, and have it to the full.

How has your understanding of this verse developed through your time in *Waking the Dead*, and in this guidebook? What do you understand better now about the offer of Jesus to us—and what do you better understand about the *context* of that offer?

Let's review the Four Streams again before we see how they work together. Describe them in your own words, and why they are crucial to the Christian life.

Walking with God

Receiving His Intimate Counsel

Deep Restoration

Spiritual Warfare

Let me come back now to Stephen's story and use it to show how the Four Streams work together to set us free. You might recall that I asked Stephen to first tell me his story. We need to hear a person's story to get some understanding and context of what's going on in their heart and life. This is the stream of Counseling. I always listen carefully for the wounds, for how we mishandle them, and for where the Enemy has probably come in. Stephen's wounds had a clear theme to them (as do ours). In his case, it was betrayal and abandonment. (pp. 169–70)

Are you seeing the themes of the wounds, the "incidents," the assault, and the misunderstanding that your heart has endured over the years? Describe those themes.

If not, it might be good to take some time aside—maybe a weekend away at a cabin—to pray and ask Jesus to reveal your own story to you. Or it might help to lay out your story to another person, get his or her insight and perspective.

But there is another piece of evidence that we often overlook. As we began to help Stephen, there was a strong pull on me to drop him altogether, a vague but strong sense that felt like, *C'mon, John. This isn't worth it. You can't help him. Back off.* In other words, betray and abandon him. The Enemy will always try to get you to do to someone what he is doing to that person. I've seen this *so* many times. A woman came into my office and immediately I felt this pull toward lust and *Use her—she's available.* Her story centered around the wounds of sexual abuse. That's where the Enemy had a stronghold. A man came in with a deep wound of emasculation. *Despise him* was the pull, and it took a serious conscious effort not to do so. There is a gravitational field the Enemy creates around a person that pulls everyone in her life to do to her what he is doing to her. Heads up—it's not you, and being aware of it becomes a *very* helpful diagnostic. (p. 170)

Okay, this idea of a "pull" you feel toward another person is just huge. I wish I'd given a whole chapter to it, because it really is a very, very helpful guide in seeing what the attack is on another person. Take a moment and list a handful of the key people in your life: family, friends, coworkers. Can you name what it is that you often want to do to them?

And what about you—what do you feel people are so often doing to you? Is it dismiss you, or maybe shame you, or look to you to solve everything? Can you see in what they are doing what the Enemy is doing against your heart?

We prayed and listened to God on behalf of Stephen—listening to God, walking with God throughout the entire process, as his disciples. Jesus confirmed that there were spirits of Betrayal and Abandonment pinning down his heart, along with a spirit of Desolation. (Anytime someone totally loses his sense of God, can't worship, can't pray, loses faith, Desolation is usually a part of things.)

Yes—spirits have personalities and specific functions. Michael (whose name means "who is like God?") is an archangel, the captain of the Lord's hosts, with special duties to protect God's people (Rev. 12:7; Dan. 10:13, 21). Gabriel's name means "strong man of God," and he is often given the role of messenger (Dan. 8:16;

Luke 1:19, 26). Fallen angels have similar qualities, though twisted for evil. Jesus rebukes a "deaf and mute spirit" from a boy (Mark 9:25), and Legion from a tormented man (Mark 5:1–13). Paul casts out from a fortune-teller a spirit of divination (Acts 16:18). (pp. 170–71)

This might be a really new thought to you—that there are all sorts of foul spirits out there with all sorts of "personalities" or special sins they are experts in. What do you make of this?

To Clarify

Again, the knowledge of the spiritual realm has practically been stripped away from our modern, scientific era. We do not even think about it most of the time. But that doesn't make it go away. It might help you to review some of these biblical passages to begin to understand the spiritual realm—the rest of reality. Look up the passages I cited in the last section to see the angelic and demonic world described. In addition, consider . . .

Daniel 7:9–10 and Rev 5:11

Daniel and John get a glimpse into the spiritual realm, and what they see are "ten thousand times ten thousand" angels. That's 100,000,000. And that's just the number they *saw*! There's a whole bunch of 'em.

Rev 12:4

Satan swept "a third of the stars out of the sky and flung them to the earth." This is the passage that leads us (and commentators as diverse as John Milton and Charles Ryrie) to believe that one-third of the angels fell with Satan. If it happened before John saw the 100,000,000 good angels around the throne of God, it means there are about 50,000,000 fallen angels (or foul spirits) in the

Enemy's service. Even if you take one-third from 100,000,000, it gives you about 33,000,000. In other words, a whole lot of angels in Satan's army.

Rev 12:9

Satan is hurtled to the earth, "and his angels with him." So when you hear someone say, "Satan is really attacking me," it's probably not Satan himself but one of his workers. Most of the time, we are attacked by some member of his army. Satan himself usually has bigger fish to fry.

But remember: though Satan has a large army bent on our destruction, God's angels still outnumber them by at least two to one!

Now I know—there is a great deal of debate today around the issue of a Christian's being "possessed" by a demon. I am not saying that Stephen was possessed. I am saying that there were spiritual enemies present in his life—set *against* him, trying to make an illegitimate claim over him. Paul teaches in Ephesians that unresolved emotional issues can create spiritual strongholds in our lives—"'In your anger do not sin': Do not let the sun go down while you are still angry, and do not give the devil a foothold" (4:26–27). The word means more than just "opportunity"; it conveys a place of influence, even strong influence. The New International Version and *The Message* translate it as "foothold"; the New Living Translation has it as "mighty foothold." Paul is not writing about non-Christians; he is clearly speaking to believers and he is making it clear that we can have demonic footholds in our lives. (p. 171)

TO CLARIFY

This principle for Ephesians 4:26–27 is actually a very helpful thing to know—that your struggles in a certain arena such as lust or anger or discouragement may not be all your fault. It makes it really hard to hope for victory if we think it's just us, that we are "blowing it." To discover that the Enemy is trying to capitalize on some weakness in your life means that by getting rid of *him*, you have a much better chance of overcoming the weakness.

In other words, instead of just blaming yourself and "trying harder," you have a much better chance for victory if you act as though you are in a world at war, and resist the Enemy as Scripture tells you to do.

Think again about those recurring struggle areas in your life. What are they? Name them.

Can you see in those areas you listed here a related wound, or some event in your story that helps to put them in context? As a man, Stephen struggled with Betrayal and Abandonment. Looking at his story, you can see why—abandoned by his father at age three, "abandoned" by his mom in her death (and, he thought, by God). Abandoned and betrayed by two of his closest friends. How might the Enemy have taken an opportunity in your life to make those struggles even harder to overcome?

That is why, before we could go after those enemies of Stephen's heart, he first had to confess his part in the mess. God honors our will (remember God's words to Catherine—"you do it"). Stephen had to renounce the vow he'd made as a young boy never to let anyone get close to him again. Childhood vows are very dangerous things; they act as major agreements with the Enemy, give him permission to enter some part of our lives. Stephen also had to confess the bitterness he held toward God for not saving his mother, and toward those two men who had betrayed him.

(Bitterness is one example of "letting the sun go down" on an issue, and giving the devil a foothold.) By bringing those sins under the blood of Christ, the Enemy lost his hold (Col. 2:13–15; Rev. 12:11).

Now, the apostle Peter teaches us, *we* are to resist the devil because he "prowls around like a roaring lion looking for someone to devour" (1 Peter 5:8). Not just tempt. *Devour.* That idea has a vicious connotation to it, as in "really harm." Maul. And Peter goes on to clarify that this "someone" includes Christians because he says we are to "resist him, standing firm in the faith, because you know that your brothers throughout the world are undergoing the same kind of sufferings" (v. 9). He is writing to Christians, and using other Christians as examples that we can and will be spiritually assaulted—sometimes in very vicious ways. We *must* resist. (p. 171)

We must do it. We must resist. And not just once, but as with Catherine of Sienna, it might take a week or a month or more.

First, bring each of those struggle areas now to Christ. Confess your part in them (you have a will, you have made choices). Bring it all under the blood of Jesus, which cleanses you from every sin (1 John 1:9).

Then, resist your Enemy. Tell Satan and his workers that they have no claim in your life. Resist them, out loud. Tell them to flee. Get *fierce*!

It was time for us to get fierce. Time for the stream of Warfare. You'll notice that sometimes Jesus had to command foul spirits with a *stern* voice (Luke 4:35). In fact, when he first tried to deliver the man with Legion in him, the demon didn't leave— and *Christ* was doing the commanding! He had to get more information, in that case, the name and number of the demons present (Mark 5:1–13).

Now, I know—setting people free from demonic oppression might seem really weird to our modern, scientific world, but it has been a normal part of Christian ministry ever since Jesus modeled it for us. (Remember—things are not what they seem. We are at war.) The disciples made it an essential part of their ministry too. "Crowds gathered from the towns around Jerusalem, bringing their sick and those tormented by evil spirits, and all of them were healed" (Acts 5:16). The early church fathers saw it as an essential part of their ministry too. Listen to this prayer, one of

many deliverance prayers penned by John Chrysostom, archbishop of
Constantinople:

> Satan, the Lord rebukes you by his frightful name! Shudder, tremble, be
> afraid, depart, be utterly destroyed, be banished! You who fell from heaven and
> together with you all evil spirits: every evil spirit of lust, the spirit of evil . . . an
> imaginative spirit, an encountering spirit . . . or one altering the mind of man.
> Depart swiftly from this creature of the Creator Christ our God! And be gone
> from this servant of God, from his mind, from his soul, from his heart, from
> his reins, from his senses, from all his members, that he might become whole
> and sound and free, knowing God.

Notice that Saint John is rebuking foul spirits by name, on behalf of a believer
("this servant of God"). One at a time, we brought the authority of Jesus Christ, who
is Lord, and the fullness of the Cross, Resurrection, and Ascension against all three
foul spirits set against Stephen. We commanded them to release their claim on him,
and to go to their judgment in the name of Jesus. After a fierce battle, they left.
Stephen was free. (pp. 172–73)

To Clarify

What are you feeling this moment? Is it fear, or intimidation? Is it that old
sense of *I don't really think I want to go here; this spiritual warfare stuff is creepy*?
Or maybe *This doesn't apply to me—I think I'll just skip over this stuff.* Where do
you suppose *that* is coming from?

But that was not the end of the work for Stephen.

We then turned to the issue of his broken heart. We moved from the stream of
Warfare to the stream of Healing, for to leave those places unhealed is only to invite
the Enemy to return in another form, another day. We prayed with Stephen in the
way I described at the end of Chapter 8, bringing the broken places into the healing
presence of Jesus. It was dramatic, it was beautiful, and *it worked*. He is writing music
again, hearing God's voice, and starting another fellowship group. He is free. (p. 173)

Oh, how beautiful it is to see someone come to freedom in Christ. To see his heart come out from under the rubble, and his glory begin to shine.

At this point in your journey, how is your heart doing? Where do you think you need the various streams in your life?

FIFTEEN MINUTES TO FREEDOM

A few years ago, as Stasi and I really began to wake up and have our eyes opened to the spiritual battle raging against us and those we love, she said, "Quick little prayers just aren't going to do it anymore." I'm smiling and shaking my head as I recall this. How true it was; how true it has become. If we would do what Jesus did—heal all those who are under the power of the devil—and if we would find the life that he offers us, we have to fight for it. Fiercely. That is where we are now in this great Story.

. . . So what I offer here is a walk through the prayer that Stasi and I, and our ministry team, pray every day . . . It might seem a bit more involved than the prayer most of us shoot up to God as we run out the door, but I promise you, this is fifteen minutes toward *freedom*! Quick little prayers aren't going to do it anymore. (pp. 173–74)

As a close to this chapter, why don't you take some time to look up each Scripture reference that I've provided for the prayer in the footnotes? You'll find it very encouraging!

Then take a few moments to pray through the daily prayer. Go slowly, and really put your heart into it. If you find yourself distracted, stop, back up to where you were last focused, and continue.

My dear Lord Jesus, I come to you now to be restored in you—to renew my place in you, my allegiance to you, and to receive from you all the grace and mercy I so desperately need this day. I honor you as my sovereign Lord, and I surrender every aspect of my life totally and completely to you. I give you my body as a living sacrifice; I give you my heart, soul, mind, and strength; and I give you my spirit as well.

. . . I cover myself with your blood—my spirit, my soul, and my body. And I ask your Holy Spirit to restore my union with you, seal me in you, and guide me in this time of prayer. In all that I now pray, I include [my wife, and/or my children, by name]. Acting as their head, I bring them under my authority and covering, and I come under your authority and covering. Holy Spirit, apply to them all that I now pray on their behalf.

. . . Dear God, holy and victorious Trinity, you alone are worthy of all my worship, my heart's devotion, all my praise and all my trust and all the glory of my life. I worship you, bow to you, and give myself over to you in my heart's search for life. You alone are Life, and you have become my life. I renounce all other gods, all idols, and I give you the place in my heart and in my life that you truly deserve. I confess here and now that it is all about you, God, and not about me. You are the Hero of this story, and I belong to you. Forgive me, God, for my every sin. Search me and know me and reveal to me any aspect of my life that is not pleasing to you, expose any agreements I have made, and grant me the grace of a deep and true repentance.

. . . Heavenly Father, thank you for loving me and choosing me before you made the world.[1] You are my true Father—my Creator, my Redeemer, my Sustainer, and the true end of all things, including my life. I love you; I trust you; I worship you. Thank you for proving your love for me by sending your only Son, Jesus, to be my substitute and representative.[2] I receive him and all his life and all his work, which you ordained for me. Thank you for including me in Christ,[3] for forgiving me my sins,[4] for granting me his righteousness,[5] for making me complete in him.[6] Thank you for making me alive with Christ,[7] raising me with him,[8] seating me with him at your right hand,[9] granting me his authority,[10] and anointing me with your Holy Spirit.[11] I receive it all with thanks and give it total claim to my life.

. . . Jesus, thank you for coming for me, for ransoming me with your own life.[12] I honor you as my Lord; I love you, worship you, trust you. I sincerely receive you as my redemption, and I receive all the work and triumph of your crucifixion, whereby I am cleansed from all my sin through your shed blood,[13] my old nature is removed,[14] my heart is circumcised unto God,[15] and every claim being made against me is disarmed.[16] I take my place in your cross and death, whereby I have died with you to sin and to my flesh,[17] to the world,[18] and to the Evil One.[19] I am crucified with Christ, and I have crucified my flesh with all its passions and desires.[20] I take up my cross and crucify my flesh with all its pride, unbelief, and idolatry. I put off the old man.[21] I now bring the cross of Christ between me and all people, all spirits, all things. Holy Spirit, apply to me (my wife and/or children) the fullness of the work of the crucifixion of Jesus Christ for me. I receive it with thanks and give it total claim to my life.

. . . Jesus, I also sincerely receive you as my new life, my holiness and sanctification, and I receive all the work and triumph of your resurrection, whereby I have been raised with you to a new life,[22] *to walk in newness of life, dead to sin and alive to God.*[23] *I am crucified with Christ, and it is no longer I who live but Christ who lives in me.*[24] *I now take my place in your resurrection, whereby I have been made alive with you,*[25] *I reign in life through you.*[26] *I now put on the new man in all holiness and humility, in all righteousness and purity and truth. Christ is now my life,*[27] *the one who strengthens me.*[28] *Holy Spirit, apply to me [my wife and/or my children] the fullness of the resurrection of Jesus Christ for me. I receive it with thanks and give it total claim to my life.*

. . . Jesus, I also sincerely receive you as my authority and rule, my everlasting victory over Satan and his kingdom, and I receive all the work and triumph of your ascension, whereby Satan has been judged and cast down,[29] *his rulers and authorities disarmed,*[30] *all authority in heaven and on earth given to you, Jesus,*[31] *and I have been given fullness in you, the Head over all.*[32] *I take my place in your ascension, whereby I have been raised with you to the right hand of the Father and established with you in all authority.*[33] *I bring your authority and your kingdom rule over my life, my family, my household, and my domain.*

And now I bring the fullness of your work—your cross, resurrection, and ascension—against Satan, against his kingdom, and against all his emissaries and all their work warring against me and my domain. Greater is he who is in me than he who is in the world.[34] *Christ has given me authority to overcome all the power of the Evil One, and I claim that authority now over and against every enemy, and I banish them in the name of Jesus Christ.*[35] *Holy Spirit, apply to me (my wife and my children) the fullness of the work of the ascension of Jesus Christ for me. I receive it with thanks and give it total claim to my life.*

. . . Holy Spirit, I sincerely receive you as my Counselor, my Comforter, my Strength, and my Guide.[36] *Thank you for sealing me in Christ.*[37] *I honor you as my Lord, and I ask you to lead me into all truth, to anoint me for all of my life and walk and calling, and to lead me deeper into Jesus today.*[38] *I fully open my life to you in every dimension and aspect—my body, my soul, and my spirit—choosing to be filled with you, to walk in step with you in all things.*[39] *Apply to me, blessed Holy Spirit, all of the work and all of the gifts in pentecost.*[40] *Fill me afresh, blessed Holy Spirit. I receive you with thanks and give you total claim to my life (and my wife and/or children).*

. . . Heavenly Father, thank you for granting to me every spiritual blessing in the heavenlies in Christ Jesus.[41]

I receive those blessings into my life today, and I ask the Holy Spirit to bring all those blessings into my life this day. Thank you for the blood of Jesus. Wash me once more with his blood from every sin and stain and evil device. I put on your armor—the belt of truth, the breastplate of righteousness, the shoes of the readiness of the gospel of peace, the helmet of salvation. I take up the shield of faith and the sword of the Spirit, the Word of God, and I wield these weapons against the Evil One in the power of God. I choose to pray at all times in the Spirit, to be strong in you, Lord, and in your might.[42]

Father, thank you for your angels. I summon them in the authority of Jesus Christ and release them to war for me and my household.[43] *May they guard me at all times this day. Thank you for those who pray for me; I confess I need their prayers, and I ask you to send forth your Spirit and rouse them, unite them, raising up the full canopy of prayer and intercession for me.*[44] *I call forth the kingdom of the Lord Jesus Christ this day throughout my home, my family, my life, and my domain. I pray all of this in the name of Jesus Christ, with all glory and honor and thanks to him.*

We've been praying along these lines for several years now. Every time we do it's like a fog lifting—the clouds break, and suddenly, faith is obvious, God is near, we see again, and we can breathe. Give it a week or two—you'll see. (p. 180)

Do it. Give it a week or two, and see!

NOTES

1. Ephesians 1:4.
2. Romans 5:8.
3. 1 Corinthians 1:30.
4. Colossians 2:13.
5. 2 Corinthians 5:21.
6. Colossians 2:10.
7. Colossians 2:13.
8. Colossians 3:1.
9. Ephesians 2:6.
10. Luke 10:19; Ephesians 2:6.
11. Ephesians 1:13.
12. Matthew 20:28.
13. 1 John 1:9.
14. Colossians 2:11.
15. Romans 2:29.
16. Colossians 2:15.
17. Romans 6:11.
18. Galatians 6:14.
19. Colossians 1:13.
20. Galatians 2:20.
21. Ephesians 4:22.
22. Romans 6:4.
23. Romans 6:11.
24. Galatians 2:20.
25. Ephesians 2:5.
26. Romans 5:17.
27. Colossians 3:4.
28. Philippians 4:13.
29. John 12:31.
30. Colossians 2:15.
31. Matthew 28:18.
32. Colossians 2:10.
33. Ephesians 2:6.
34. 1 John 4:4.
35. Luke 10:19.
36. John 14:16; Acts 9:31.
37. Ephesians 1:13.
38. John 15:26; 16:13.
39. Galatians 5:25.
40. Ephesians 4:8.
41. Ephesians 1:3.
42. Ephesians 6:10–18.
43. Hebrews 1:14.
44. 2 Corinthians 1:8–11.

In the second film of *The Lord of the Rings* trilogy—*The Two Towers*—there is a king who is reluctant to go to war. Theoden, lord of the horse warriors of Rohan, is fearful and timid. An army is marching through his lands, an army bred for a single purpose: to destroy the world of men. Villages fall; women and children are slain. Still Theoden balks: "I will not risk open war." "Open war is upon you," says Aragorn, "whether you would risk it or not." As I watched this scene I could not help thinking of the church. It made me so sad. I love the Bride of Christ. I hate to see her captive in any way. *The primary reason* most people do not know the freedom and life Christ promised is that they won't fight for it, or they have been told not to fight for it. Friends, we are now in the midst of an epic battle, a brutal and vicious war against an Enemy who knows his time is short. Open war is upon you, whether you would risk it or not. (p. 181)

And so, where is your heart as you end this chapter? Can you put into a sentence or two what God has said to you through this chapter?

What do you need to do for your heart and your freedom?

PART FOUR

The Way of the Heart

Rise, heart
Thy Lord is risen.
—George Herbert

If all of this is true (and it is true), there are some deep and urgent implications. Many of those have probably begun to occur to you already. But there are two I must unveil.

You might remember that the first Christians were called "followers of the Way" (Acts 9:2; 18:25–26). They had found the Way of Life and had given themselves over to it. They lived together, ate together, fought together, celebrated together. They were intimate allies; it was a fellowship of the heart. How wonderful it would be if we could find the same. How dangerous it will be if we do not.

Finally, let me ask you a question: How would you live differently if you believed your heart was the treasure of the kingdom? Because we are at war, the business of guarding the heart is a most serious business indeed. It is precisely because we do not know what the next turn of the page will bring that we nourish our hearts *now*, knowing at least this much: we will need our whole hearts for whatever is coming next. Above all else, you must care for your heart. For without your heart . . . well, have a look around. (pp. 183–84)

CHAPTER ELEVEN

FELLOWSHIPS OF THE HEART

All the believers were one in heart.

—LUKE THE PHYSICIAN (ACTS 4:32)

HEART MONITOR

How's your heart today?

For you to be fully alive is to be . . . ?

To guard your heart requires you to . . . ?

Your role in God's Larger Story is . . . ?

What is the Adversary currently doing to assault your heart?

FIRST REACTION

What was the effect of this chapter upon you? Write out your impressions: any new or challenging thoughts, emotions or stirrings in your heart, or even perhaps something you intend to do.

A MYTHIC PARABLE

Elrond summoned the hobbits to him. He looked gravely at Frodo. "The time has come," he said.

"The Company of the Ring shall be Nine; and the Nine Walkers shall be set against the Nine Riders that are evil. With you and your faithful servant, Gandalf will go; for this shall be his great task, and maybe the end of his labors. For the rest, they shall represent the other Free Peoples of the World: Elves, Dwarves, and Men. Legolas shall be for the Elves; and Gimli son of Glóin for the Dwarves. They are willing to go at least to the passes of the mountains, and maybe beyond. For men you shall have Aragorn son of Arathorn, for the Ring of Isildur concerns him closely."

"Strider!" cried Frodo. "Yes," he said with a smile. "I ask leave once again to be your companion, Frodo." "I would have begged you to come," said Frodo, "only I thought you were going to Minis Tirith with Boromir." "I am," said Aragorn. "And the Sword-that-was-Broken shall be re-forged ere I set out to war. But your road and our road lie together for many hundreds of miles. Therefore Boromir will also be in the Company. He is a valiant man."

"There remain two more to be found," said Elrond. "These I will consider. Of my household I may find some that it seems good for me to send." "But that will leave no place for us!" cried Pippin in dismay. "We don't want to be left behind. We want to go with Frodo." "That is because you do not understand and cannot imagine what lies ahead," said Elrond. "Neither does Frodo," said Gandalf, unexpectedly supporting Pippin. "Nor do any of us see clearly. It is true that if these hobbits understood the danger, they would not dare to go. But they would still wish to go, or wish they had dared, and be shamed and unhappy. I think, Elrond, that in this matter it would be well to trust rather to their friendship than to great wisdom."

"Let it be so, then. You shall go," said Elrond, and he sighed. "Now the tale of Nine is filled. In seven days the company must depart." (J. R. R. Tolkien, *The Fellowship of the Ring*) (pp. 185–86)

What does it stir in you—awaken you to?

❈ THE BIG IDEAS

FIRST, we must not live alone. *You must not go alone.* You must have a fellowship of the heart.

SECOND, the fellowship we need must be small. Though we are part of a great company, we are meant to live in little platoons. The little companies we form must be small enough for each of the members to know one another as friends and allies.

THIRD, the fellowship we need must be intimate. The sort of devotion we want and need takes place within a shared life.

FOURTH, this is something we will have to fight for.

Big Idea 1: WE MUST NOT LIVE ALONE

Once more, lend a mythic eye to your situation. Let your heart ponder this:

> You awake to find yourself in the middle of a great and terrible war. It is, in fact, our most desperate hour. Your King and dearest Friend calls you forth. Awake, come fully alive, your good heart set free and blazing for him and for those yet to be rescued. You have a glory that is needed. You are given a quest, a mission that will take you deep into the heart of the kingdom of darkness, to break down gates of bronze and cut through bars of iron so that your people might be set free from their bleak prisons. He asks that you heal them. Of course, you will face many dangers; you will be hunted. (pp. 186–87)

By now we hope you see that this is our situation. Quickly respond: What does this stir in you? Where's it taking you? What's going on in your heart right now?

> *It's the clarity of the context of my life that I need about twenty-four times a day . . . my heart resonates with the reality that I have no insignificant role in God's larger story. It's what I've always hoped to be true about my life. (Craig)*

Would you try to do this *alone*? (p. 187)

> *Do chickens bark? The scale of God's story and the guile of the opposition requires a multitude of brave-hearted souls teaming together. So much of my story has been "going it alone." I want to be a part of a larger story, so large it requires others to live in it. I yearn to be among a band of like-minded warriors. (Craig)*

To what degree has your Christian journey felt like a solo? If it has been a solo journey, what do you lack from not having others engaged with you?

What impact does going it alone have upon you, your mission, and others? And why have you gone it alone?

For some, you have tried to go it alone—and been taken out—and you may now be ready to be a part of a good fellowship. Others of you have not had a good experience in a fellowship; thus, you'd rather go it alone and suffer the consequences instead of endure again the emptiness or pain of a fellowship group. Do either of these fit your experience?

Something stronger than fate *has* chosen you. Evil *will* hunt you. And so a Fellowship *must* protect you. Honestly, though he is a very brave and true hobbit, Frodo hasn't a chance without Sam, Merry, Pippin, Gandalf, Aragorn, Legolas, and Gimli. He has no real idea what dangers and trials lie ahead. The dark mines of Moria; the Balrog that awaits him there; the evil orcs called the Urak-hai that will hunt him; the wastes of the Emyn Muil. He will need his friends. And you will need yours. You must cling to those you have; you must search wide and far for those you do not yet have. *You must not go alone.* From the beginning, right there in Eden, the Enemy's strategy has relied upon a simple aim: divide and conquer. Get them isolated, and take them out. (p. 187)

Which posture are you currently in?

1. Clinging to those you have. How could this group be even more the group you desire?

2. Searching for those you don't yet have. What are you doing—really—to bring it together?

3. Neither. Why?

> You see this sort of thing at the center of every great story. Dorothy takes her journey with the Scarecrow, the Tinman, the Lion, and of course, Toto. Prince Caspian is joined by the last few faithful Narnians, and together they overthrow the wicked king Miraz. Though in the eyes of the world they are only gladiator-slaves, walking dead men, Maximus rallies his little band and triumphs over the greatest empire on earth. When Captain John Miller is sent deep behind enemy lines to save Private Ryan, he goes in with a squad of eight rangers. And, of course, Jesus had the Twelve. This is written so deeply on our hearts: *You must not go alone.* The Scriptures are full of such warnings, but until we see our desperate situation, we hear it as an optional religious assembly for an hour on Sunday mornings. (pp. 187–88)

Given your schedules, pressures, and all the options, what would it take either to get into a group or to push the group you're in to new heights?

Is the circle of Christians that make up your fellowship essential to the living out of your life? Is your group indispensable to your spiritual survival and growth? Are you desperate for your times together? Could it be different?

For the first time in my life, "Yes" feels like the right and true answer. It has been a very long time coming. (Craig)

Think again of Frodo, or Neo, or Caspian, or Jesus. Imagine you are surrounded by a small company of friends who know you well (characters, to be sure, but they love you, and you have come to love them). They understand that we are all at war, know that the purposes of God are to bring a man or woman fully alive, and are living by sheer necessity and joy in the Four Streams. They fight for you, and you for them. Imagine you *could* have a little fellowship of the heart. Would you want it if it were available? (p. 188)

Would you want this, if it were available?

Yes, I've always wanted it and want it more than ever now. (Craig)

Big Idea 2: THE FELLOWSHIP WE NEED MUST BE SMALL

Though we are part of a great company, we are meant to live in little platoons. The little companies we form must be small enough for each of the members to know one another as friends and allies. Is it possible for five thousand people who gather for an hour on a Sunday morning to really and truly *know* each other? Okay, how about five hundred? One hundred and eighty? It can't be done. They can't possibly be intimate allies. It might be fun and encouraging to celebrate with a big ol' crowd of people, but who will fight for your heart? (pp. 190–91)

How would you describe the level of relationship you have experienced in your fellowship?

Superficial: external; sharing is basically limited to information, clichés, kind disinterest, being "nice." Acquaintance/friend.

Personal: deeper; sharing fears, emotions, desires, and disappointments; authentic; interactive engagement; committed to growth. Ally.

The Four Streams are something we learn, and grow into, and offer one another, within a small fellowship. We hear each other's stories. We discover each other's glories. We learn to walk with God together. We pray for each other's healing. We cover each other's back. This small core fellowship is the essential ingredient for the Christian life. Jesus modeled it for us *for a reason*. Sure, he spoke to the masses. But he *lived* in a little platoon, a small fellowship of friends and allies. His followers took his example and lived this way too: "They broke bread in their homes and ate together with glad and sincere hearts" (Acts 2:46); "Aquila and Priscilla greet you warmly in the Lord, and so does the church that meets at their house" (1 Cor. 16:19); "Give my greetings to the brothers at Laodicea, and to Nympha and the church in her house" (Col. 4:15). (p. 191)

Given that we need to live in the Four Streams, where will you go to find them?

Who, if it were possible, would you want in your fellowship? Can you think of specific individuals? What about each of them is attractive?

If so, begin to pray about initiating a gathering of these like-hearted souls.

If not . . . where does you heart go in disappointment? Loneliness? Despair? Hopelessness?

This now becomes one of the passions of your prayer life. "God, I ask you to provide, to raise up a few allies who will join me in guarding our hearts and fighting for the hearts of others. Give me eyes to see these people. I give you this desire and trust your provision."

> When Scripture talks about church, it means *community*. The little fellowships of the heart that are outposts of the kingdom. A shared life. They worship together, eat together, pray for one another, go on quests together. They hang out together, in each other's homes. When Peter was sprung from prison, "he went to the house of Mary the mother of John" where the church had gathered to pray for his release (Acts 12:12).
>
> . . . You simply cannot be devoted to a mass of people; devotion takes place in small units, just as in a family. (p. 192)

How is it that we have come to be warehoused in Sunday services with people we do not really know, for an hour a week, separated for the rest of our days of real living, and call that *church*? You might have a guess who pulled *that* off on us.

How does the description of church vary from your experience of church? How do you react to this description: It involves too much? There's not enough time for that kind of involvement? It was appropriate in a less hectic culture/time . . . ?

My understanding of church has been "the bigger, the better." Size was a sign of health. I remember the saying "Numbers count because people count," as if attracting a crowd would result in people's being transformed into fully alive followers of Christ. We believed a large church would provide services a smaller church couldn't, and it did, kinda. We had a great youth and children's ministry; this kept adults coming, however, they were dying by droves from the lack of any of the Four Streams functioning. Thousands gathered, sitting next to people they never knew, week after week, to be "inspired" out of their spiritual malaise and exhorted to be more involved in activities that were well intended, but largely unfruitful by biblical standards. Me, I'm ready for something vastly different. (Craig)

Now, I'm not suggesting you don't do whatever it is you do on Sunday mornings. I'm simply helping you accept reality—whatever else you do, you *must* have a small fellowship to walk with you and fight with you and bandage your wounds. Remember, the path is narrow, and *few* find it. *Few* means small in number, as opposed to, say, massive. This is essential. This is what the Scriptures urge us to do. First. Foremost. Not as an addition to Sunday. *Before* anything else. (pp. 192–93)

To Clarify

Each Christian should select his church because he is convinced that within its particular structure he will find the greatest opportunities for spiritual growth, the greatest satisfactions for his human needs, and the greatest chance to be of helpful service to those around him. (Billy Graham)

Big Idea 3: THE FELLOWSHIP WE NEED MUST BE INTIMATE

Of course, small groups have become a part of the programming that most churches offer their people. For the most part, they are short-lived. There are two reasons. First, you can't just throw a random group of people together for a twelve-week study of some kind and expect them to become intimate allies. The sort of devotion we want and need takes place within a shared life . . .

I love this description of the early church: "All the believers were one in heart" (Acts 4:32). A camaraderie was being expressed there, a bond, an esprit de corps. It means they all loved the same thing, they all wanted the same thing, and they were bonded together to find it, come hell or high water. And hell or high water *will* come, friends, and this will be the test of whether or not your band will make it: if you are one in heart . . . My goodness—churches split over the size of the parking lot or what instruments to use during worship. Most churches are *not* "one in heart."

Second, most small groups are anything but redemptive powerhouses because, while the wineskin might be the right size, they don't have the right wine. You can do some study till you're blue in the face, and it won't heal the brokenhearted or set the captive free. We come; we learn; we leave. It is not enough. Those hearts remain buried, broken, untouched, *unknown.* It is the Way of the Heart and the Four

Streams that turns a small fellowship into a redemptive community. It is knowing that you are at war, that God has chosen you and evil is hunting you, and so a fellowship like Frodo's must protect you. How many small groups have you been a part of where what we did for Leigh is what happens all the time? (pp. 193–94)

For many of us, a small, intimate group is scary; others find it attractive. Describe the kind of fellowship—its activities, mission, personality, values—that you would very much enjoy being apart of.

Read the story of Leigh on pages 188–90 and the account of the Fellowship meeting on pages 185–86. Do you see how vital a small, intimate circle of people who are willing and desire to fight for one another's hearts is? Is something akin to this appealing?

It's so appealing, and so foreign to my experience that I have to fight off the discouraging suggestion that I may never know such a fellowship . . . Dear Christ, gift me with such a group. Amen. (Craig)

Pray for the vitality and life of the group you're in, or pray that God would form such a group for you.

It is a royal mess. I will not whitewash this. It is *disruptive*. Going to church with hundreds of other people to sit and hear a sermon doesn't ask much of you. It certainly will never expose you. That's why most folks prefer it. Because community will. It will reveal where you have yet to become holy, right at the very moment you are so keenly aware of how *they* have yet to become holy. It will bring you close and you will be *seen* and you will be *known,* and therein lies the power and therein lies the danger. Aren't there moments when all those little companies, in all those stories, hang by a thread? Galadriel says to Frodo, "Your quest stands upon the edge of a knife. Stray but a little and it will fail, to the ruin of all. Yet hope remains while the Company is true." (p. 197)

Why is real fellowship so messy? Why is it so difficult for us to gather and develop the intimacy required to be the group we must be?

> Because the people are messy: they talk too much or not at all; they can be boring, superficial, or way too deep; they need help (moving, financially, guidance, counseling, parenting, marital, spiritual) that requires more time, energy, or insight than I may have (their real-life problems often don't link with a single clear and helpful passage of Scripture). We often lack common interests (I don't want to go to the opera or rodeo; they don't want to go out in bad weather or discuss a newly released CD). Fellowship is so messy because it requires more of me than I either feel I have or want to give. Having said that, I want to be in an environment that requires God to come through . . . for me and others. And my true, good heart does want to fight for others. (Craig)

Big Idea 4: THIS IS SOMETHING YOU WILL HAVE TO FIGHT FOR

We've experienced incredible disappointments in our fellowship. We have, every last one of us, hurt one another. Sometimes deeply . . .

. . . Seriously, now—how often have you seen this sort of intimate community work? It is *rare.* Because it is hard, and it is fiercely *opposed.* The Enemy hates this sort of thing; he knows how powerful it can be, for God and his kingdom. For our hearts. It is devastating to him. Remember divide and conquer? Most churches survive because everyone keeps a polite distance from the others. We keep our meetings short, our conversations superficial . . . We have settled for safety in numbers—a comfortable, anonymous distance. An army that keeps meeting for briefings, but never breaks into platoons and goes to war. (pp. 197–98)

So, if your fellowship group experience has been short of what God intended it to be, what or who was at fault? Was it the direction of the group? The people? You? The Enemy? Or some combination?

Are you prepared for the Enemy's resistance to your fellowship? Where is the resistance going to come?

There are two things you now have that you didn't have before, and they enable this sort of fellowship to work. First, your heart is good, and the others' hearts are good. This makes it so much easier to trust and to forgive. Whatever may be happening in the moment, whatever the misunderstanding might be, I know that our hearts toward one another are good, and that we are for each other. Craig says something that stings. If I thought, *You know, he meant that; he's trying to hurt me,* it would pretty quickly trash the relationship. But I know that is not his heart toward me; that is not who he truly is. If I thought it were, why, I'd turn tail and run. (pp. 198–99)

Why would knowing our hearts are good help us understand and love one another?

Second, we know we are at war. The thought that says, *Oh, brother, here goes Frank again. Why can't he just drop it about his mother? What is it with these people? They're not really my friends. I'm outta here.* That's the Enemy. You *must* remember that the Enemy is always trying to pull everyone else to do to you what *he* is doing to you. As I said earlier, he creates a kind of force field, a gravitational pull around you that draws others into the plot without their even knowing it. Gary walks in the room and, suddenly, I'm irritated at him. It's not me, and it's not him. I have to know that. His lifelong assault has been, "If you can't get it right, we don't want to be with you." It's a lie. It's the Enemy. I don't feel that way toward him *really*. But unless I live with this awareness, keep a watchful eye out for it, and resist, I'll get sucked into the pull, start making agreements with it, and there goes the friendship. (p. 199)

Why would knowing that we are at war help us understand and love one another?

A true community is something you'll have to fight for. You'll have to fight to get one, and you'll have to fight to keep it afloat. But you fight for it as you bail out a life raft during a storm at sea. You want this thing to work. You *need* this thing to work. You can't ditch it and jump back on the cruise ship. This *is* the church; this is all you have. Without it, you'll go down. Or back to captivity. (p. 199)

Is this passion to fight rising in you? Describe why or why not.

Be careful about what you are looking for from community. For if you bring your every need to it, it will collapse. Community is no substitute for God. I left our annual camping trip absolutely exhausted and disappointed. As we drove home, I realized it was because I was looking to them to validate me, appreciate me, fill this aching void in my heart. Only once in ten days did I take time to be away with God, alone. I was too busy trying to get my needs met through them. Which is why community cannot live without solitude.

I was so struck by the layout of the early Irish and Scottish monasteries when we visited there last year. First, they knew they *had* to live in community. They needed each other. But in every single location, set apart from the community buildings by about a twenty-minute walk, you'd find little "cells," small stone huts designed for one member to get alone and be with God. They knew community could not survive without solitude. There is a rhythm to life together, as Bonhoeffer said. We first go to God, alone, so that we have something to bring back to the community. This is part of lifestyle warfare. I know my community needs me; they are coming over tonight. So I'd better get with God this afternoon. I want to contribute. I want to play a vital role. (pp. 200–201)

Why is solitude so important for us and for the community we're in? Which is true: solitude drives community, or community drives solitude?

I can't get from the community, no matter how good it is, the validation, hope, strength, and personal direction I can only get from God. (Craig)

God is calling together little communities of the heart, to fight for one another and for the hearts of those who have not yet been set free. That camaraderie, that intimacy, that incredible impact by a few stouthearted souls—that is available. It is the Christian life as Jesus gave it to us. It is completely normal. (p. 203)

And so, where is your heart as you end this chapter? Can you put into a sentence or two what God has said to you through this chapter?

I pant, crave, yearn, desire, covet, thirst, and hunger for churches to be the Church. Oh, dear God, work in me and through me to encourage the development of redemptive communities, churches that will walk deeply with you and fight for the hearts of others. Amen. (Craig)

What do you need to do for your heart and your freedom?

CHAPTER TWELVE

LIKE THE TREASURES OF THE KINGDOM

Arise, shine, for your light has come,
*   and the glory of the LORD rises upon you.*
See, darkness covers the earth
*   and thick darkness is over the peoples,*
but the LORD rises upon you
*   and his glory appears over you.*
                    —ISAIAH (60:1–2)

HEART MONITOR

For you to be fully alive is to be . . . ?

To guard your heart requires you to . . . ?

Your role in God's Larger Story is . . . ?

What is the Adversary currently doing to assault your heart?

FIRST REACTION

THE TRUEST STORY OF THEM ALL

Jesus, once more deeply moved, came to the tomb. It was a cave with a stone laid across the entrance. "Take away the stone," he said. "But, Lord," said Martha, the sister of the dead man, "by this time there is a bad odor, for he has been there four days." Then Jesus said, "Did I not tell you that if you believed, you would see the glory of God?" So they took away the stone. Then Jesus looked up and said, "Father, I thank you that you have heard me. I knew that you always hear me, but I said this for the benefit of the people standing here, that they may believe that you sent me." When he had said this, Jesus called in a loud voice, "Lazarus, come out!" The dead man came out, his hands and feet wrapped with strips of linen, and a cloth around his face. Jesus said to them, "Take off the grave clothes and let him go." (John 11:38–44)

And when Jesus had cried out again in a loud voice, he gave up his spirit. At that moment the curtain of the temple was torn in two from top to bottom. The earth shook and the rocks split. The tombs broke open and the bodies of many holy people who had died were raised to life. They came out of the tombs, and after Jesus' resurrection they went into the holy city and appeared to many people. (Matt. 27:50–53) (pp. 204–5)

What does this story stir in you?

❋ THE BIG IDEAS

FIRST, our hearts are a treasure to be cared for. How kind of God to give us this warning, like someone entrusting to a friend something precious to him, with the words: "Be careful with this—it means a lot to me."

SECOND, caring for our own hearts isn't selfishness; it's how we begin to love. What will we bring to others if our hearts are empty, dried up, pinned down? Love is the point. And we can't love without our hearts, and we can't love well unless our hearts are well.

THIRD, caring for our hearts is how we protect our relationship with God.

FOURTH, caring for our hearts is your first blow against spiritual warfare.

Big Idea 1: OUR HEARTS ARE A TREASURE TO BE CARED FOR

"Above all else, guard your heart" (Prov. 4:23). We usually hear this with a sense of "keep an eye on that heart of yours," in the way you'd warn a deputy watching over some dangerous outlaw, or a bad dog the neighbors let run. "Don't let him out of your sight." Having so long believed our hearts are evil, we assume the warning is to keep us out of trouble. So we lock up our hearts and throw away the key, and then try to get on with our living. But that isn't the spirit of the command at all. It doesn't say guard your heart because it's criminal; it says guard your heart because it is the wellspring of your life, because it is a *treasure*, because everything else depends on it. How kind of God to give us this warning, like someone entrusting to a friend something precious to him, with the words: "Be careful with this—it means a lot to me."

Above all else? Good grief—we don't even do it once in a while. We might as well leave our life savings on the seat of the car with the windows rolled down—we're that careless with our hearts. "If not for my careless heart," sang Roy Orbison, and it might be the anthem for our lives. Things would be different. I would be farther along. My faith would be much deeper. My relationships so much better. My life would be on the path God meant for me . . . if not for my careless heart. We live completely backward. "All else" is above our hearts. I'll wager that caring for your heart isn't even a category you think in. "Let's see—I've got to get the kids to soccer, the car needs to be dropped off at the shop, and I need to take a couple of hours for *my* heart this week." It probably sounds unbiblical, even after all we've covered.

Seriously now—what do you do on a daily basis to care for your heart? Okay, that wasn't fair. How about weekly? *Monthly?* (pp. 207–8)

Yeah, so what do you do to care for your heart? Have you viewed it as God does . . . as a treasure?

What was the last thing you did that really refreshed your heart—and why did it?

I got up early in the morning, went for a walk as the sun was rising, and simply enjoyed the beauty of the morning, the moist, woodsy smell of the pine trees, the light breeze, and the stillness that set the rhythm for my heart that day. God was present, I could see him, hear him, and share all that surfaced in my soul. (Craig)

Take a chunk of time to ask prayerfully—and perhaps specifically—"What would caring for my heart right now, at this time in my life, look like?" (This is a prayer that would be good to pray on a regular basis.)

God intends that we treat our hearts as the treasures of the kingdom, ransomed at tremendous cost, as if they really *do* matter, and matter deeply . . .

> If then you are wise, you will show yourself rather as a reservoir than as a canal. A canal spreads abroad water as it receives it, but a reservoir waits until it is filled before overflowing, and thus without loss to itself [it shares] its superabundant water. (Bernard of Clairvaux)

A beautiful picture. The canal runs dry so quickly, shortly after the rains subside. Like a dry streambed in the desert. But a reservoir is a vast and deep reserve of life. We are called to live in a way that we store up reserves in our hearts, and *then* offer from a place of abundance. As Jesus said, "Every teacher of the law who has been instructed about the kingdom of heaven is like the owner of a house who brings out of his storeroom new treasures as well as old" (Matt 13:52). I'm thinking, *Storeroom? What storeroom?* "The good man brings good things out of the good stored up *in his heart* . . . For out of the overflow of his heart his mouth speaks" (Luke 6:45, emphasis added). (p. 209)

How full is your storeroom? If you are a "canal," are you aware of your lack of reserves? Does the thought of being a reservoir appeal to you? What would such a change require?

At this very moment, I feel more like a canal. Until this question, I wasn't aware of my lack of reserves . . . it's been a distractingly busy season. I'm amazed at and disappointed in my ability to go for great lengths on fumes. I truly want to see my heart as the treasure it really is, then care for it by nurturing it with beauty, silence, reflection, music, adventure, and reading. (Craig)

If you are a reservoir, how have you done it? What do you have to resist or battle to maintain your overflow?

Did you know that God gives out of the *abundance* of his heart? One of the first things John tells us about his dear friend Jesus is that "from the fullness of his grace we have all received one blessing after another" (John 1:16). From God's *fullness,* we receive blessing. Or as Paul prays in Ephesians, "I pray that out of his glorious riches he may strengthen you" (3:16), which is to say, out of the riches God has stored up in his great heart, he gives to ours. Dallas Willard reminds us,

> He is full of joy. Undoubtedly he is the most joyous being in the universe.
> The abundance of his love and generosity is inseparable from his infinite joy.
> All of the good and beautiful things from which we occasionally drink
> [Willard includes the sea in all its beauty, or a wonderful movie, or music] . . .
> God continuously experiences in all their breadth and depth and richness.

> Has it ever occurred to you that God is such a loving and generous person *because* his heart is filled, like a reservoir, with joy? It is because his heart is brimming with good things and experiences that God is able to love and forgive and suffer so long for mankind. The same holds true for us. Are you a delight to be with after an hour in traffic? No wonder we are so short on grace and mercy. Life drains us dry—and we just accept it as the normal way to live. (pp. 210–11)

What situations may expose how dry you really are—traffic, your teen, an annoying colleague, your spouse? Again, what does your heart need to be a reservoir?

Shamefully, I admit it's probably when I'm with my wife, Lori, or my daughters. I'll give to others and expect a free pass on being present, engaged, and offering myself at home. It's at home that I'm exposed as dry. (Craig)

We were really burned out, Stasi and I, when we headed off to this year's annual family vacation. Before we left, she told me she was "done with people." I was too. Even a short conversation felt draining. Neither of us wanted to see anyone. We gave some serious thought to becoming hermits. Enough of this community stuff. Living alone in a hut in the Kalahari sounded like paradise. God's remedy was eight days in southeast Alaska, photographing grizzly bears, sea kayaking with humpback whales, eating more than our share of great food, and taking in breathtaking views in every direction. We got home late on a Saturday night; I woke Sunday morning to hear Stasi chatting away on the phone with a friend. She called another, and another, all day long. "Just catching up," she said with a smile. (p. 211)

How would you live differently if you believed your heart was the treasure of the kingdom?

I intend to frequently ask myself and God, "What does my heart need?" without any restrictions on the possible answers. I'll slow down, take more walks, listen to God, make the effort to journal more and to articulate my feelings, desires, hopes, and pains. I'll read God's Word to find God instead of finding "stuff." I'll write more letters, dance more, cry more, eat less. Given the reality of the battle, I'll fight for my heart. Given the truth of my good heart, I'll trust it more. (Craig)

Big Idea 2: CARING FOR OUR OWN HEARTS ISN'T SELFISHNESS; IT'S HOW WE BEGIN TO LOVE

Yes, we care for our hearts for the sake of others. Does that sound like a contradiction? Not at all. What will you bring to others if your heart is empty, dried up, pinned down? Love is the point. And you can't love without your heart, and you can't love well unless your heart is well. (p. 211)

Currently, what does your heart offer to those closest to you? What would you like to offer them?

My heart is offering enough to maintain relationship . . . not to lose ground. I'm pretty much engaged and listening; I care, but I am not anxious to go deep and heavy (I'm tired, and in need of some rest and renewal). I'm letting some relational yellow flags slide but intend to come back to them later (they'll still be there, right?). I'm smiling, nice, and for the most part offering about 60 percent of myself to others. Hey, that's up 10 percent from last week!

    I'd like to care for my heart to such an extent that others will be getting pretty close to 100 percent of who I am and what I have to offer. I'd like to move out of a maintenance mode and gain ground in my relationships more than I have recently. (Craig)

How often do you think you are weak or ill equipped to live out the Christian life when in fact it's not your inability, it's your good-yet-empty heart that is the cause?

> When it comes to the whole subject of loving others, you must know this: how you handle your own heart is how you will handle theirs. This is the wisdom behind Jesus urging us to love others *as we love ourselves* (Mark 12:31). "A horrible command," as C. S. Lewis points out, "if the self were simply to be hated." If you dismiss your heart, you will end up dismissing theirs. If you expect perfection of your heart, you will raise that same standard for them. If you manage your heart for efficiency and performance, that is what you'll pressure them to be. (pp. 211–12)

They are right. Listen to Oswald Chambers:

> There are people you come in contact with who "freeze" you—you cannot think, things do not "go," everything feels tight and mean; you come into the zones of other people and all

those bands disappear—you are surprised at how clearly you can think, everything seems to "go" better. You take a deep breath and say, "Why, I feel quite different; what has happened?" The one personality brought an atmosphere that froze the heart . . . kept it cold, kept it down; kept it back. The other personality gave the heart a chance to expand.

You know those folks. You've experienced people who either live from the heart or don't . . . and the permission or denial their example gives you.

How do you think you treat your own heart? Are you aware of it?

I'm becoming more aware that my history of caring for my heart is similar to the way I care for my car . . . when the "idiot lights" go on, I take care of the problem; otherwise I assume everything is peaches and cream. (Craig)

If you were to get honest answers from those close to you, what would they say about how you treat their hearts? Do they "freeze" around you, or do they feel free? Now react to the idea that you treat your heart exactly the same way.

Yes, there is a place for sacrifice. And yes, I know, a lot of very selfish things have been done under the excuse that "I'm taking care of my heart." I've heard divorces and affairs justified that way. But the fact that someone abuses an idea doesn't make it a bad idea. People overeat too. Does that mean you shouldn't enjoy eating? Some pretty awful things have been done in the name of Christianity. Does that mean you shouldn't be a Christian? Don't let others' bad choices shape your life. Care for your heart. With all diligence. Above all else. Not only for your own sake; not even primarily for your own sake. Do it in order to love better, for the sake of those who need you. (p. 212)

Big Idea 3: CARING FOR YOUR HEART IS HOW YOU PROTECT YOUR RELATIONSHIP WITH GOD

Now there's a new thought. But isn't our heart the new dwelling place of God? It is where we commune with him. It is where we hear his voice. Most of the folks I know who have never heard God speak to them are the same folks who live far from their hearts; they practice the Christianity of principles. Then they wonder why God seems distant. *I guess all that intimacy with God stuff is for others, not me.* It's like a friend who hates the telephone. He neglects to pay the bills, could care less when the phone company disconnects the service. Then he wonders why "nobody ever calls." You cannot cut off your heart and expect to hear from God. (p. 213)

If God seems distant, maybe the issue isn't with him, but with a neglected heart. Do you know this to be true from personal experience?

What's the difference between protecting your relationship with God and striving to develop or maintain your relationship? And which has been your orientation?

The same holds true for those folks who cannot seem to find the abundant life Christ promised. Your heart is where that life flows into you. "On the last and greatest day of the Feast, Jesus stood and said in a loud voice, 'If anyone is thirsty, let him come to me and drink. Whoever believes in me, as the Scripture has said, streams of living water will flow from within him'" (John 7:37–38). "Flow from within" means "from your inmost being," from your heart, that wellspring of life within you. God *wants* to give you his life; your part is to keep the channel open. You do that by caring for your heart. (p. 213)

How does this change your attitude toward caring for your heart?

> We care for ourselves in the same way a woman who knows she is deeply loved cares for herself, while a woman who has been tossed aside tends to "let herself go," as the saying goes. God's friends care for their hearts because they matter to *him*. (p. 213)

If you can't bring yourself to do it for your own sake, or for the sake of those who have to live with you, then for God's sake, do it.

> What does your heart need? In some sense it's a personal question, unique to our makeup and what brings us life. For some it's music; for others it's reading; for still others it's gardening. Our friend Lori loves the city; I can't wait to get out of one. Bart reads articles on flying; Cherie loves a good novel. Bethann loves horses, and Gary needs time working in the woodshop. You know what makes your heart refreshed, the things that make you come alive. I don't get the thing with women and baths, but I know that Stasi loves them and finds a little retreat in a fifteen-minute tub. "He leads me to soak in bubbly waters." For me and the boys it's the dirtier, the happier.
>
> Yet there are some things all hearts have in common. We need beauty; that's clear enough from the fact that God has filled the world with it . . .
>
> . . . We need to drink in beauty wherever we can get it—in music, in nature, in art, in a great meal shared. These are all gifts to us from God's generous heart. Friends, those things are not decorations to a life; they bring us life. (p. 214)

Where do you go for beauty? What music is good for your heart? When and where do you go for nature, art?

Vistas, the woods, a stream, the beach, a park, a garden, museums and art galleries, art and nature photographic journals. Stormy weather stirs me, a good red wine and conversation with intimate allies renews me, praying as I drive nowhere in the presunrise morn awakens me. The music I love ranges, depending on my mood/heart, from classic sixties rock to dramatic instrumental movie sound tracks to classical . . . And lying on a couch in a semiconscious state of prayer is heaven for my soul. (Craig)

We need silence and solitude. Often. Jesus modeled that, though few of us ever follow his example. Not even one full chapter into the gospel of Mark, there's quite a stir being created by the Nazarene. "The whole town gathered at the door," which is to say, Jesus is becoming the man to see. Let's pick up the story there:

> That evening after sunset the people brought to Jesus all the sick and demon-possessed. The whole town gathered at the door, and Jesus healed many who had various diseases . . . Very early in the morning, while it was still dark, Jesus got up, left the house and went off to a solitary place, where he prayed. Simon and his companions went to look for him, and when they found him, they exclaimed: "Everyone is looking for you!" Jesus replied, "Let us go somewhere else." (1:32–38).

"Everyone is looking for you!" Surely you can relate to that. At work, at home, at church, aren't there times when everything seems to come down on you? Now this is a tremendous opportunity. I mean, if Jesus really wants to launch his ministry, increase sales, expand his audience, this sure looks like the chance to do it. What does he do? He leaves. He walks away. Everyone is looking for you! Oh, really . . . then we'd better leave. It cracks me up. Wendell Berry might have been writing of Jesus when he said, "His wildness was in his refusal—or his inability—to live within other people's expectations." We are just the opposite; our entire lives are ruled by the expectations of others, and when you live like that, the heart is always the first thing to go. (pp. 215–16)

Are silence and solitude a part of your life? What benefits to *your* heart would they bring? What do you do to get away, or what could you do, for seasons of silence and solitude?

A simple starting place would be to ask God. *What do you have for my heart?* You'll be stunned by what he guides you into.

. . . You might not think God wants this for you . . . but have you asked him? I think I've missed thousands of little promptings over the years, simply because I wasn't open to the fact that they occur. But I am astounded and more than a little humbled by the number of gifts he has given my heart since I've begun to give even partial heed to Proverbs 4:23. And I know I'm not some special case. (pp. 216–17)

Take time now, and in a quiet spirit ask God, "What do you have for my heart?" What did you hear?

What is your heart longing for?

Now, the Enemy will tell you this is foolish. *There are so many more important things to do. You can get to it some other time. You're being selfish. This isn't even what you want, anyway.* Remember: he fears you—fears your heart's coming alive and full and free. Caring for your heart is an act of obedience. It is an act of love, an act of faith, an act of war. (p. 217)

Big Idea 4: CARING FOR YOUR HEART IS YOUR FIRST BLOW AGAINST SPIRITUAL WARFARE

The heart that is weak is vulnerable. Are you able to fend off accusation when you are wiped out from a hard week? It seems so true at that point, and who really cares anyway? Listen—the first wave of any strike against us is to rob us of the heart to fight it. It always starts that way, with that sense of being too tired or overwhelmed. Heads up—the main assault is coming on the heels of it. Facing an overwhelming enemy at Agincourt, King Henry prays for his men, that the opposing numbers will not "pluck their hearts from them."

It works like this: hyenas cannot bring down a lion in its prime. What they do is run it and taunt it and wear it down to the point of exhaustion. Once they see it cannot defend itself, then they close in. The strategy of our Enemy in the age we live in now is *busyness* or *drivenness*. Ask the people you know how things are going. Nine out of ten will answer something to the effect of "really busy." Every time I call another ministry I get voice mail. "They're busy right now, can I put you into voice mail?" The deadly scheme is this: *keep them running. That way, they'll never take care of their hearts. We'll burn them out and take them out.* (p. 218)

Without using others as a reference point, but instead using the criteria of how you want to live and what is good for your heart, answer these questions: Are you driven? Too busy?

Read the Iwo Jima story on pages 219–220. What would a swim be for you?

CONCLUSION

> We now are going to war. This is the beginning of the end. The hour is late, and you are needed. We need your heart. (p. 220)

Let that sink in. You are needed. Your heart is desperately needed. Your thoughts?

> If there were something more I could do to help you see, I wish to God I could have done it. Tears fill my eyes for fear that I have not done enough. You must turn, then, back to myth—tomorrow and the next day and the next. Read the battle of Helms Deep; it's chapter 7 of *The Two Towers*. Watch any of the trilogy of those films. And the opening of *Gladiator*. That is where we are now. Or if you can bear it, watch the battle of the Ia Drang Valley in *We Were Soldiers*. It is so deeply true to what we must face, will face. Linger over the climax of *The Prince of Egypt*, where God goes to war against Egypt to set his people free. If the images of the Exodus do not move you, I don't know what will.
>
> Read Lewis's last installment in *The Chronicles of Narnia*, titled *The Last Battle*. I don't think even he knew all he was saying there. These stories and images are among the stories that God is giving to his people for this hour. They are gifts to us from his hand, clarity and strength for our hearts. Apparently, we need them. They will do you a great good. And then . . . you will do a great good. Remember our friends from the Emmaus Road? Well, the story ends with their eyes wide open. They go tearing back to Jerusalem, their hearts bursting. "They found the Eleven and those with them, assembled together and saying, 'It is true!'" (Luke 24:33–34). It is true. All of it.
>
> We are now far into this epic Story that every great myth points to. We have reached the moment where we, too, must find our courage and rise up to recover our hearts and fight for the hearts of others. The hour is late, and much time has been wasted. Aslan is on the move; we must rally to him at the stone table. We must find Gepetto lost at sea. We must ride hard, ride to Helm's Deep and join the last great battle for Middle Earth. Grab everything God sends you. (pp. 220–21)

What are those stories that speak so deeply to your heart? And *why* do they?

When will you go get them and let them nourish you?

FINAL GUIDANCE

We want you to carry on now, continue to care, to guard, and to fight for your heart. Here are some suggestions:

- Get a journal to record your journey in. Write out the words God speaks to you concerning his heart for you, regarding your calling and place in his Larger Story. Reread and review past notes and words regularly.
- Pray the Daily Prayer on pages 223–26 regularly.
- Live with these questions:

God, what would you like to say or speak to me concerning at this moment?

What does my heart need?

For me to be fully alive is to be . . . ?

What do I believe to be true about the relationships and circumstances I'll face today?

God has called me to . . . ?

In what ways is the Adversary attempting to steal the wonderful work of God in or through me?

"Until the day dawns and the morning star rises in your *hearts*" (2 Peter 1:19, emphasis added).

Yes. Until the day dawns, friends, and the Morning Star rises in all our *hearts*. (p. 221)

WILD AT HEART: A BAND OF BROTHERS

Five friends. Eight days. No scripts. Here's what it looks like to live the message of *Wild at Heart* in a band of real brothers. John and his band of brothers spent eight days shooting this series on a ranch in Colorado. Horses. Rappelling. White-water rafting. Fly-fishing. And some of the most honest conversation you will ever hear from men. This is not a scripted instructional video. It is real life and conversation shared with the cameras rolling. If you're looking for more, this is the next step in the *Wild at Heart* adventure for you and your band of brothers. The Multi-Media Facilitator's Kit includes John's best-selling *Wild at Heart* hardcover book; the *Wild at Heart Field Manual*; the *Wild at Heart Facilitator's Guide*; the video teaching series available either in VHS or DVD format; and a media kit to help you get the word out so others can join your band of brothers.

ISBN 0-7852-6278-4

WILD AT HEART

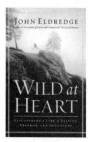

Every man was once a boy. And every little boy has dreams, big dreams. But what happens to those dreams when they grow up? In *Wild at Heart*, John Eldredge invites men to recover their masculine heart, defined in the image of a passionate God. And he invites women to discover the secret of a man's soul and to delight in the strength and wildness men were created to offer.

Hardcover—ISBN 0-7852-6883-9
Abridged Audio in 3 CDs—ISBN 0-7852-6298-9
Abridged Audio in 2 Cassettes—ISBN 0-7852-6498-1
Spanish Edition (*Salvaje de Corazón*)—ISBN 0-8811-3716-2

THE WILD AT HEART JOURNAL

This rugged leather-bound guided journey will help men explore their hearts and journal their adventures. This includes totally different material than that found in the *Field Manual*.

ISBN 0-8499-5763-X

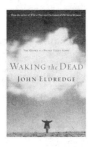

WAKING THE DEAD

In *Waking the Dead*, John Eldredge shows how God restores your heart, your true humanity, and sets you free. There are four streams, Eldredge says, through which you can discover the abundant life: Walking with God, Receiving His Intimate Counsel, Deep Restoration, and Spiritual Warfare. And once the "eyes of your heart" are opened, you will embrace three eternal truths: Things are not what they seem; This is a world at war; and You have a crucial role to play. A battle is raging. And it is a battle for your heart.

Hardcover—ISBN 0-7852-6553-8
Abridged Audio in 3 CDs—ISBN 0-7852-6299-7

A GUIDEBOOK TO WAKING THE DEAD: *Embracing the Life God Has for You*

In a style similar to *The Journey of Desire Journal and Guidebook*, Eldredge and Craig McConnell lead you on a journey toward a restored heart, true humanity, and ultimate freedom.

ISBN 0-7852-6309-8

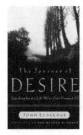

THE JOURNEY OF DESIRE.

Author Dan Allender calls *The Journey of Desire* "a profound and winsome call to walk into the heart of God." This life-changing book picks up where *The Sacred Romance* leaves off and continues the journey. In it, John Eldredge invites you to abandon resignation, to rediscover your God-given desires, and to search again for the life you once dreamed of.

Hardcover Edition—ISBN 0-7852-6882-0
Trade Paper Edition—ISBN 0-7852-6716-6

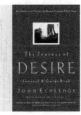

THE JOURNEY OF DESIRE JOURNAL AND GUIDEBOOK

John Eldredge, with Craig McConnell, offers a unique, thought-provoking, and life-recapturing workbook, which invites you to rediscover your God-given desire and to search again for the life you once dreamed of. Less of a workbook and more of a flowing journal, this book includes personal responses to questions from John and Craig.

ISBN 0-7852-6640-2

THE SACRED ROMANCE

This life-changing book by Brent Curtis and John Eldredge has guided hundreds of thousands of readers from a busyness-based religion to a deeply felt relationship with the God who woos you. As you draw closer to Him, you must choose to let go of other "less-wild lovers," such as perfectionistic drivenness and self-indulgence, and embark on your own journey to recover the lost life of your heart and with it the intimacy, beauty, and adventure of life with God.

Trade Paper Edition—ISBN 0-7852-7342-5
Special Collector's Edition (Hardcover)—ISBN 0-7852-6723-9
Abridged Audio—ISBN 0-7852-6786-7
Spanish Edition (*El Sagrado Romance*)—ISBN 0-8811-3648-4

THE SACRED ROMANCE WORKBOOK AND JOURNAL

John Eldredge offers a guided journey of the heart featuring exercises, journaling, and the arts to usher you into an *experience*—the recovery of your heart and the discovery of your life as part of God's great romance.

ISBN 0-7852-6846-4

THE THREE CLASSICS

The Sacred Romance, The Journey of Desire, and *Wild at Heart* are available in one specially priced package. Whether this set is for yourself, to replace the dog-eared and penciled-in copies you already own, or is a gift to share John's powerful message with someone you love, these *Three Classics from John Eldredge* will continue to give long after they are received.

ISBN 0-7852-6635-6

DARE TO DESIRE

Complete with beautiful, full-color design, *Dare to Desire* is the perfect book if you are ready to move beyond the daily grind to a life overflowing with adventure, beauty, and a God who loves you more passionately than you dared imagine. With brand-new content as well as concepts from *The Sacred Romance, The Journey of Desire,* and *Wild at Heart,* John Eldredge takes you on a majestic journey through the uncharted waters of the human heart.

ISBN 0-8499-9591-4